D0521151

Chameleons

Chameleons
Their Care and Breeding

Linda J. Davison

ISBN 0-88839-353-9
Copyright © 1997 Linda J. Davison

Cataloging in Publication Data
Davison, Linda J.
    Chameleons

    ISBN 0-88839-353-9

    1. Chameleons.   2. Chameleons as pets.   I. Title.
QL666.L23D38 1995   639.3'95   C95-910744-4

All rights reserved. No part of this publication may be reproduced, stored in
a retrieval system or transmitted, in any form or by any means, electronic,
mechanical, photocopying, recording, or otherwise, without the prior
written permission of Hancock House Publishers.
Printed in Hong Kong—Colorcraft

Editor: Nancy Miller
Production: Lorna Brown
Cover design: Lorna Brown
Front cover photograph: David Adamson

Published simultaneously in Canada and the United States by

HANCOCK HOUSE PUBLISHERS LTD.
19313 Zero Avenue, Surrey, BC V4P 1M7
(604) 538-1114   Fax (604) 538-2262
HANCOCK HOUSE PUBLISHERS
1431 Harrison Avenue, Blaine, WA 98230-5005
(604) 538-1114   Fax (604) 538-2262

Contents

Acknowledgments

I want to thank everyone who made this book possible. Without your faith in me, along with your support, this tremendously hard work would have been impossible. Thank you!

Thanks to the pioneers in the field of chameleon conservation, Don Wells (our lucky charm), Bob Mailloux (at Sandfire Dragon Ranch), Dr. Whalen, D.V.M., Dr. Stahl, D.V.M., photographers Les Birgham, David Adamson and Don Wells, graphic artist Shelly Short, editor Julia Norquist, Beth Duggan Benneck (for the very first edit and for toughening my skin), Rob and Mimi Velton (for the preliminary editing), David Hancock (for giving a crazy housewife a chance to fulfill a dream), the Coblers, the Hilberts, my supportive friends and my family. A special thanks to my girls, who have put up with mom always working and dad always doing mom's old jobs, I love you lots! And last but not least, my husband Stephen. Without his compulsive shopping and outrageous personality this journey would not have been possible.

Introduction

Chameleons is my attempt to supply information to a new and growing group of chameleon lovers. The fascination with these wonderful, colorful and captivating creatures is worldwide, and it is an addiction which I fell into quite by accident. "*Chamaeleo* fever" is spreading with such speed that nothing seems to be able to stop it. My husband Stephen provides a good example of how people afflicted by this disease behave. He purchased our first chameleon (Johnston's chameleon), amid protests from me because I knew I would get stuck taking care of this little ugly! I always suspected that Stephen was certifiable, but when he bought this animal it reinforced my resolve to call the nearest psychiatrist. After thinking the matter through however, I just knew that this newfound fascination would soon wear off and things would be back to normal. But an amazing thing happened. My husband, who would rather watch TV than read, started looking for any information he could get his hands on, which at that time wasn't much.

Caring for this lizard obsessed him. He questioned breeders, pet store owners, hobbyists or anyone who seemed to know anything about chameleons. The information he did find in books, written by pioneering experts, was often outdated, contradictory or inaccurate. This surprised me, and piqued my interest.

Soon, and unbeknownst to me, the oak lumber for my long-awaited entertainment center was being cut up and turned into a large vivarium (a man-made habitat for reptiles) with a simulated lava-like backdrop, lavish foliage, a waterfall and a pair of Jackson's chameleons (*Chamaeleo jacksonii xantholophus*) to further the insult. These animals were so happy in their new surroundings that they began to mate and produce offspring. This soon fascinated me—suddenly I had the fever!

Occasionally someone would call and say, "I know where to get a couple of Panther chameleons for a good price. Do you want them?" My husband would look to me, keeper of the check book, and I would reply, "Can we afford not to buy them?" I couldn't believe I would ever be caught uttering these words! Soon we had a pair of Parson's chameleons, followed by the Madagascar giant chameleons (*C. oustaleti* and *C. verrucosus*, respectively) and so on, until we were overrun with this preoccupation.

As our thirst for knowledge reached a fever pitch, word spread fast of our addiction, and soon people were parading through our house. The squeals of the frightened as they fled from our temple of doom were quite amusing. This made an occasional cricket in the night shirt, or my toddler handing me only half of a cricket, a little more bearable. It is a fact that you haven't lived until one of your neighbors catches you running around like a lunatic through a local field catching insects with a butterfly net.

In a typical scenario, an average Joe goes into ABC Pet Store and sees a horned creature walking with agonizing slowness up a hanging plant. Fascinated, Joe wants to know what it is. Before the store owner has a chance to explain much about this enticing animal, Joe has his check book out and is saying, "I gotta have it." Joe is sent home with an information sheet listing some suggested reading, and little else. If Joe is typical, his new pet will survive only a couple of weeks in a small aquarium with a bowl of water, a plastic plant, and a light bulb. From this experience, Joe concludes that keeping a chameleon is worth neither the expense nor the trouble. Next time he'll get a cat.

Few people truly comprehend that in the next few years if the present trend continues, the little rain forest that is left for many of these animals will be gone. All chameleons are on the CITES threatened list (Convention on International Trade in Endangered Species of wild flora and fauna). Many species will never reach the endangered species list before they become extinct.

Chameleons are not only for the advanced reptile keeper as previously thought. I believe people can easily be taught to keep and breed chameleons in captivity. There are hundreds of people who have already proven this to be true. In southern California alone, a small group of chameleon breeders annually produces several thousand captive-reared animals. Within this small group, the combined experience of housing and breeding these animals totals twenty years plus. I think the skeptics are wrong. Who knows more about chameleons in captivity than breeders who have hatched three, four or more generations? With trust, admiration and respect, I have collected the knowledge of this small group of chameleon breeders as well as others and combined it with my own experiences to form the backbone of this book. My husband and I are now the owners of Sticky Tongue Farms in southern California, which is the largest chameleon farm in the world. Now it is time to share what we have learned with others who have the fever.

1

Chameleons in Nature

Most chameleons come from Africa and the island of Madagascar, with a few species native to southern Europe, Saudi Arabia and India. With such a range of temperatures and climates, it is naive to place all chameleons into a group requiring a hot, dry climate, as is commonly believed.

These animals can be found high in the cool, moist Uluguru Mountains of Tanzania, and the hot plains of Madagascar's high deserts. Approximately 40 percent of the chameleons are native to Madagascar, which is the fourth largest island in the world.

Many chameleons are now being protected in national parks and reserves, such as those in Cameroon, Tanzania and on Nosy Be Island, the big island off the northwestern coast of Madagascar.

Genus Classification

Classification of true chameleons has been a topic of much debate for many years. Scientists are still arguing about which genus each species should be placed under, based on evolved physical traits such as the structure of the lungs or hemipenis. I am not qualified to argue these points on a scientific level.

What is agreed upon by all scientists is that chameleons are in the class Reptilia, and the order Squamata. This order consists of three main families: warm lizards, lizards and snakes. In the lizard subfamily Sauria, there are four main infraorders: Anguimorpha (anguid), Gekkota (gecko), Iguania (iguana), and Scincomorpha (skink). Chameleons fall into the Iguania category which consists of three main divisions:

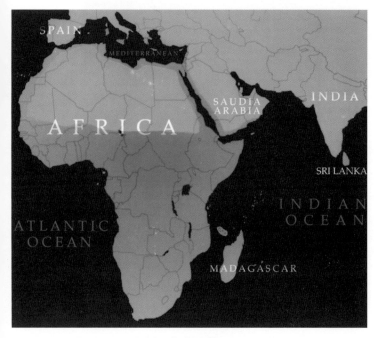

Figure 1.1: Origin of chameleons.

Figure 1.2: Head shot *Brookesia superciliaris*.

Agamids, Chameleonids and Iguanids. For our purposes we will be discussing the four most popular genera of chameleons: *Chamaeleo*, *Bradypodion*, *Brookesia* and *Rhampholeon*.

Chamaeleo

This arboreal genus has a prehensile tail which extends at least the length of the chameleon's body, snout to vent (all chameleons are described in length from tip of their snout to tip of their tail, unless stated otherwise). *Chamaeleo* consists mostly of egg-laying species. *Chamaeleo* is the largest genus, possessing the most colorful species of all chameleons. Nearly half of the species are found on Madagascar. Some grow to more than 2 feet in total length.

Bradypodion

This genus consists of dwarf species closely related to the larger *Chamaeleo*. They are also arboreal, have prehensile tails but bear live young. *Bradypodion* grow from 2–6 inches in total length.

Brookesia

This genus is commonly referred to as the pygmy stumptail group of Madagascar, as its tail is of minimal use. The species are partially terrestrial, living on the rain forest floor in the leaf litter. Usually brownish in coloration, they possess unusual scale structures. All species of *Brookesia* are egg layers, and they grow from 3–4 inches in length, with the smallest known species of chameleon being 1¼–3 inches in total length.

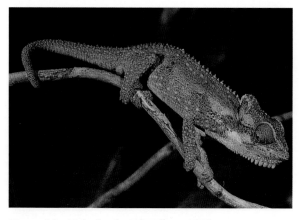

Figure 1.3: Male *Bradypodion thamnobates*.

Rhampolean

Like *Brookesia*, the chameleon of this genus is sometimes referred to as the leaf chameleons. However, they are located in Africa, mainly dwelling on the ground and in low bushes. Members of this species grow from 2–6 inches in length and are egg layers.

KINGDOM: Animalia (animals)
  PHYLUM: Cordata (chordates)
  CLASS: Reptilia (reptiles)
    ORDER: Squamata (scaled reptiles)
      FAMILIES: snakes; warm lizards; lizards
        LIZARD SUBFAMILY: Sauria
          SAURIA INFRAORDER:
          Anguimorpha; Gekkota; Iguania;
          Scincomorpha
            IGUANIA DIVISIONS:
            Agamids; Iguanids;
            Chameleonids

CHAMAELEONIDAE TABLE I

GENUS: *Brookesia*; *Rhampholeon*; *Bradypodian*; *Calumma*; *Fucifer*; *Chamaeleo*
SUBGENUS: *Chamaeleo*; *Triceros*

Figure 1.4: Female *Brookesia thieli*.

Figure 1.5: Male *Rhampholeon spectrum*.

CHAMAELEONIDAE TABLE II

GENUS: *Chamaeleo*
  MADAGASCAR SPECIES: *cucullatus; bifidus;*
    lateralis; nasutus; oustaleti; parsonii;
    rhinoceratus
  AFRICA, EUROPE and ASIA SPECIES:
    chameleon; bitaeniatus; johnstoni; oweni;
    pumilus

Anatomy of True Chameleons

Chameleons have abilities unlike any other reptile. They can rapidly change color, hang by their tails, climb trees and strike insects from afar with their tongues.

Skin

A chameleon's skin offers a wide range of textures and patterns that help to characterize different species. The composition of the skin may be smooth, warty, scaly, lumpy or any combination of textures. Their skin repels water like a freshly waxed car.

Figure 1.7: *C. labordi* female with rest coloration. This is a normal color for this chameleon.

Contrary to popular belief, chameleons do not change color to match the exact color of their surroundings. Instead, they change color due to temperature and emotional changes. This remarkably swift change is believed to occur from a shift in hormones, or a reaction by the autonomic nervous system. Color change is also a response to environmental factors such as

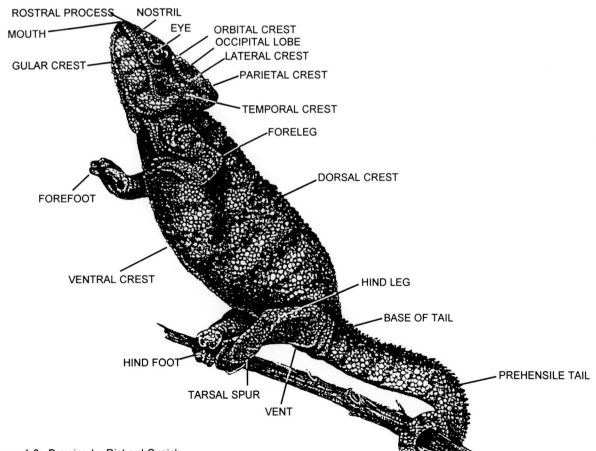

Figure 1.6: Drawing by Richard Cusick.

Figure 1.8: Female *C. labordi* in full coloration. This is a gravid or warning display to a male suitor.

Figure 1.9: Female *C. minor* in normal rest coloration.

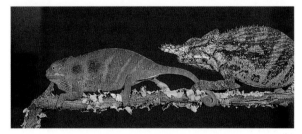

Figure 1.10: Male *C. minor* in pursuit of female.

Figure 1.11: Nonreceptive female display to pursuing male.

Figure 1.12: Female *C. minor* in full warning display color.

Figure 1.13: Battle between male and female *C. minor*.

stress, heat or cold, or a willingness to mate.

The four layers of skin which control colors are as follows:

1. The outer layer, or epidermis, consisting of transparent skin made up of keratin, much like our fingernails (this is the skin shed while the chameleon is growing).

2. The chromatophore layer, containing yellow and red pigment cells.

3. The melanophore layer containing melanin, which rises through the brownish black and red striping of this layer to cause a change in the color (the lower portion of the melanophore layer reflects blue).

4. The nether layer, which only reflects white.

When the color cells expand and shrink, a blend of these layers produces the various colors of the chameleon.

Figure 1.14: Relaxed coloration of male *C. pardalis*—Ambanja blue morph.

Figure 1.17: Male *C. quadricornis* squamation shot.

A relaxed and rested chameleon will display a muted or drab coloration. A chameleon will not display its brilliant or flashy hues unless angered, excited or stressed. Although it is possible to force a chameleon to demonstrate its brighter colors by exciting or stressing it, this kind of long-term treatment will often cause illness and eventually death.

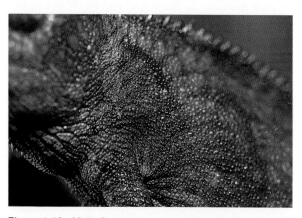

Figure 1.18: Male *C. oustaleti* squamation shot.

Figure 1.15: Male *C. pardalis*—Ambanja blue morph blanched from too high temperatures.

An excessive amount of this forced behavior is stressful to the chameleon. If the animal is displaying its normally muted color pattern it can be interpreted as a happy, relaxed display. When two males are in confrontation, the alpha male will usually become very brilliant in color and this acts as a signal to the secondary male to display only black coloration in order to show the victor it's giving in to him and wants no more aggression.

An overheated chameleon will blanch (turn paler in coloration) and a sleeping chameleon may also do this at night. While a chameleon is basking in the sun, it may turn black or very dark in order to intensify the heat rays of the sun on its body.

The term squamation refers to the scale configuration of a chameleon's skin. There are two types of patterns, which are as follows:

1. Homogeneous squamation describes scales with a consistent pattern or color.

Figure 1.16: Basking male *C. oustaleti.*

2. Heterogeneous squamation describes scales that are inconsistent in their shape.

These two terms are invaluable in species identification, as some chameleons are so closely related that a slight texture or scale shape may mean the difference between one species and another.

Eyes

Being one of the most visually dependent animals known, the chameleon's ability to see its surroundings is of utmost importance to it. Its habitat must be to its visual liking. Without the sense of security derived from what it sees, its breeding, eating and even survival are not possible.

A chameleon's vision provides its most useful tool for survival. Because of its ability to look in two different directions simultaneously, the chameleon can spot food and keep an eye out for other chameleons or predators at the same time.

Figure 1.21: Male *C. clayptratus* eye close-up.

Chameleons' eyes are an integral part of their ability to secure food. When these animals spot a food object, such as a cockroach, they will immediately focus both of their eyes upon the object, rock their bodies back and forth to judge range, and then strike at it with their tongue. They can achieve 99 percent accuracy. A one-eyed chameleon can still hunt and survive, but with a lower success rate of food capture.

Mouth

An adult chameleon's tongue can measure two-and-a-half times the length of its body when fully extended. The tongue of an infant or subadult can often reach four times the length of their body. Nature provided them with this extra length to ensure a meal. The hollow tongue is composed of three main elements: the accelerator muscles, the retractor muscles and the sticky tip. The tip is more like a toilet plunger that hits the prey hard and creates suction around it before retracting. While most insects are captured by the chameleon with its tongue, a few slippery worms and snails may be eaten by biting them

Figure 1.19: Close-up shot of eye—male *C. pardalis* blue morph.

Figure 1.20: Female *C. oshaughnessyi* eye close-up.

Figure 1.22: Male *C. oshaughnessyi* tongue shot.

Figure 1.23: Female *C. parsonii* tongue shot.

Figure 1.26: Female *C. pardalis* jaw.

Figure 1.24: Male *C. parsonii* tongue shot.

Figure 1.27: Scia dentata—male red *C. pardalis*.

Figure 1.25: Female *C. oshaughnessyi* jaw.

off a branch instead. When the tongue is not being used, it rests in the back of the throat, where it is sheathed over the hyoid bone, which is pushed up from the lower jaw like a spring to shoot the tongue at its intended prey.

In captivity, if a chameleon strikes the glass of its enclosure, or cuts its tongue causing damage, it may lose the use of it either temporarily or permanently. It will become necessary for the keeper to provide a feeding dish or, in more extreme cases, even feed by hand until the tongue is back to normal. A chameleon that has an impaired tongue is a severely handicapped creature.

A chameleon's teeth are also unique in that they are attached to the jaw bone ridge. Unlike other lizards, chameleons chew their food, often holding it for a moment in their mouth before chewing.

Scia dentata refers to the large, often white or light-colored, scales that appear to be teeth around the chameleon's lips. This resembles a skeleton and can be quite intimidating to other chameleons and predators.

Horns, Casques and Others

When defending itself, the chameleon is equipped with certain appendages such as vari-

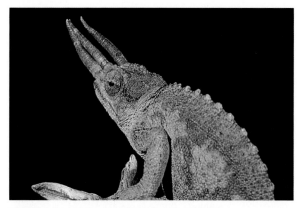

Figure 1.28: Male *C. jacksonii merumontana*.

Figure 1.31: Male *C. parsonii*'s rostral process.

Figure 1.29: *C. quadricornis* male.

Figure 1.32: Male *C. oshaughnessyi* has rostral processes like a *C. parsonii*. *Photo: David Adamson*

Figure 1.30: Male *C. clayptratus*'s impressive high casque.

ous flaps and horns as well as rapid coloration changes, physical gestures and swelling to appear larger. Many of these qualities and adornments are the tools of the trade for the males to woo potential mates. The bigger and flashier males usually get the pick of the females at mating time. The younger or less brilliant males usually have to wait their turn to breed after the dominant male or sometimes they are just out of luck altogether. The different horns, casques, crests, appendages and lobes are all helpful in species identification for us, but more importantly they serve the same purpose for the chameleons.

There are only a few true horned chameleons, and these possess annulated horns that are made up of ringlike segments consisting of bone centers wrapped in a hard keratinlike skin. Other species such as *C. fischeri* possess appendages on their noses that resemble horns, but in fact they are not. Most of the horned chameleons possess 3 horns, but *C. quadricornis* usually has

Figure 1.33: Male *C. antimena.*

Figure 1.34: Male *C. labordi* with his paddle nose.

4, and has even been known to grow as many as 6.

The different species' casques vary in shape and size depending on their individual differences. They serve not only as identification between the species but also during lean times, chameleons will store water and fat in their casques to hold them over until the return of the rainy season or until an insect happens by. The shape and height of the casques also helps water droplets to collect on them and drip into the chameleon's mouth. Some species such as *C. calyptratus* live in Yemen on the southernmost tip of the Arabian peninsula. In many parts of this country there is no measurable rainfall, therefore this species has had to adapt to another form of water collection to serve its needs. In the coastal region where this chameleon can be found, the ambient humidity approaches 100 percent. This allows the chameleon to drink dew that collects on the high casque at night and also lick moisture from the leaves in the area.

Appendages can vary in shape and size depend-

ing on the species. In some male chameleons, such as *C. fischeri*, these facial ornaments are forked, serrated and laterally compressed horn-like structures attached in front of their nose. With male *C. parsonii* there is a similar forked protuberance made up of rigidly stacked scales. Other species such as *C. antimena* have a single, laterally compressed, paddle-shaped appendage on their nose, which is soft and pliable.

Lungs

Using dissection of deceased animals, taxonomists and biologists have attempted to group chameleons into different genera according to lung shapes and sizes. Suffice to say, the different shapes and sizes of the various species' lungs tend to depict the linear evolution of these species. The lungs of many species of chameleons occupy the entire length of the body and can be quite complex, while others are more simple in their structure. The lungs can serve to help the chameleon appear larger than it really is and these lizards often inflate this large, baglike organ with air when threatened.

A chameleon's lungs are quite similar in structure to those of birds. This should not be forgotten by the chameleon keeper when constructing suitable housing for his animals. These creatures need screen enclosures that allow for constant air flow, without which they often become ill with upper-respiratory infections over a period of time. Some keepers have rigged up fans used in small computers to their lizard's glass enclosures in order to create air flow but this has also often led to upper-respiratory infection due to drafts which could have been avoided had the proper environment of a screened enclosure been provided in the first place. Certainly breeders and hobbyists are housing chameleons behind glass all over the world, but no chameleon in our care has been able to survive or breed on a long-term basis under these conditions.

Ears

Although chameleons do not have external ears like many other animals, they can hear some rudimentary sounds similar to what a nearly deaf person hears. Hearing is not one of the chameleon's better attributes, which might explain the enhanced eyesight and camouflage abilities of these animals. The ear holes lie just under the skin in approximately the same area where our ears are situated. The chameleon's auditory range is much lower than that of a human or most other higher forms of animals. Like a deaf person, a chameleon can feel the vibration from a falling branch or even the beat from music. Some chameleons "buzz" from their throat to communicate. The buzzing seems to resonates through the tree and is usually used as a warning or threat to territory invaders.

Hemipenis

Chameleons, like other lizards and snakes, have a hemipenis, which is essentially a double-lobed organ consisting of two separate penises. Only one side of this organ is useful to the animal at a time. While breeding, the animal will insert only one side of the hemipenis into the vent of the female. The sperm travel on the outside surface, usually along shallow canals and flow into her.

Chameleons have the most embellished penis of any reptile species. The organ is often covered with spiny projections arranged in different patterns and lengths depending on the species. These features allow scientists a means for species classification using the varied degree of ornate ridges, bulges and folds present to classify not only species but also the family.

Feet

A chameleon's feet and toes are very specialized for climbing trees. The toes are bundled and divided into opposing groups, with three toes inward and two toes outward on the front feet, and two toes inward and three toes outward on the back feet. This foot structure is called zygodactylous. All chameleons in the genus *Chamaeleo* have smooth-soled feet, with sharp nails and powerful grips. The smaller, ground-dwelling chameleons (such as the *Brookesia*) have spiny-soled feet.

Tail

A chameleon's tail does not grow back if it is lost, unlike that of most other lizards. Often a

Figure 1.35: Hemipenis of male red *C. pardalis.*

Figure 1.37: Male *C. melleri* with foot damage due to improper caging materials.

Figure 1.36: Hemipenis of male red *C. pardalis.*

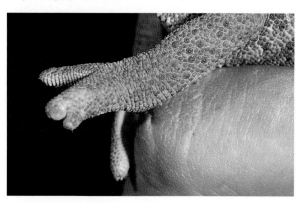

Figure 1.38: Female *C. oustaleti* with foot damage.

Figure 1.39: Close-up shot of the prehensile tail of a *C. pardalis* male Nosy Be blue morph.

Figure 1.40: Male red *C. pardalis* holding stick with his tail.

Figure 1.41: *C. malthe* male using his tail as a fifth hold.

chameleon will die as a result of trauma and stress if its prehensile tail is lost or damaged in an accident or fight with a predator.

The length of the tail usually equals the total length of the body and head. The tail acts as another "hand" to hold onto branches and supplies balance when performing tricky maneuvers. When the chameleon is walking, either on the ground or in a tree, it often holds its tail straight out behind for balance. When sleeping, the chameleon will roll its tail into a tight coil and tuck it under the body. The tail is also rolled in this fashion when the animal is comfortable and relaxed and even when showing off to a prospective mate.

Locomotion

Almost all species of chameleons move with extreme caution, often moving with a rocking motion that mimics plant leaves in a breeze. They are not easily seen in trees or shrubs, and chameleons rarely descend to the ground. When they are walking they can move at a rate of up to 20 feet per minute, making them easy prey for all kinds of animals.

There is one unique species of chameleon, *C. namaquensis*, which is in many ways a very different animal than all of the rest of the chameleons. This species has adapted to living its life on the ground surface of the South African deserts. At night it digs a hole to sleep in and feeds almost entirely on a beetle that lives in the sand dunes.

This species can move with amazing speed when compared to other chameleon species. A friend recounts a story about when he and his wife were traveling in Namibia driving on the highway and spotted a Namibian chameleon crossing the road. He stopped the car to avoid running over the animal and his wife got out to move it. When she searched for the animal both in front of and under the car it was nowhere to be seen. As she looked around she spotted the lizard making a hasty retreat into the shelter of some rubble beside the road and she set out after it in hot pursuit. The chameleon easily outdistanced her and reached the shelter with time to spare and disappeared. Our friend is very familiar with the chameleon family and was astounded at the agility and speed demonstrated by this species.

Chameleon Conservation

At present, conservation efforts to protect chameleons and their habitat as well as hundreds of other species, are being attempted in Madagascar, Tanzania and other parts of Africa. In Madagascar, on the island of Nosy Be, a reserve

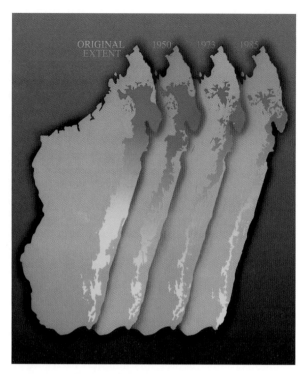

Figure 1.42: Chameleon conservation.

protects some of the range of the famous blue morph of the panther chameleon, *C. pardalis*, and other native creatures. On Madagascar other species are protected when they reside within the confines of the numerous national parks.

Tanzania and Madagascar have limited exportation of several species of chameleons in an attempt to preserve them in their natural habitat. Private land owners are also not permitting chameleons to be collected from their land, as had been done in the past.

Unfortunately, the people that reside in the countries where chameleons live are usually very poor, and have to do whatever they can to survive. This includes tragic slashing and burning of the habitats of chameleons in order to make room for farmland. In other areas, the burning of trees to make charcoal for cooking fuel (one of the peasants' main means of money making) has led to vast areas of leveled and unproductive land that was once forest. It's very difficult to tell starving people that they cannot make money or farm because chameleons and other wildlife may become extinct as a result.

This brings up yet another issue: whether the

importation of chameleons should be allowed. Some people are against importing for any reason. This is an honorable idea; however, only the last one-fifteenth of the forest habitat for chameleons is still intact in Madagascar. Photographs from space of Madagascar show the ocean is stained blood red from the huge amount of erosion of the iron-rich soils that are leaching into the ocean as a result of the deforestation of this magnificent island. If chameleons are to be saved along with the other wildlife of Madagascar, deforestation must be stopped and the people must be provided with another way to make a living. In addition, chameleons from there should be established in captivity, as a hedge against the wild population being lost due to natural and man-made catastrophes.

Captive-bred Versus Imported Chameleons

There are two sides to this issue and there will always be a controversy surrounding the taking of wild creatures from habitat for the animal trade. Some people would like to see only captive-bred chameleons being sold to the public. They feel that taking these wild-caught animals from their natural habitat is cruel and the animals should be left there to thrive or perish by whatever fate. Others believe exportation is the only hope for species survival. They believe that captive-established bloodlines will be the saving of these species for posterity.

Chameleons in the genus *Chameleo* are on the CITES list of species being watched for overexploitation, and all species need their wild populations and natural habitats to be observed by proper wildlife authorities. Unfortunately, the

Figure 1.43: Captive-bred baby red *C. pardalis*.

Figure 1.44: Captive-bred *C. verrucosus* ten minutes old.

Figure 1.45: Three-month-old male *C. verrucosus* displaying how shy these chameleons are.

Figure 1.46: Captive-bred *C. l. lateralis* baby.

Figure 1.47: Captive-bred subadult *C. pardalis*—blue morph.

governments in charge of preserving these species are also responsible for the depletion of these habitats. If no action is taken to preserve the environment, many chameleon species in the near future could conceivably only be found in the living rooms and backyards of breeders.

From what we can gather from friends and collectors in Africa and Madagascar, there are many species that are still very common and can even be found within the borders of good-sized cities.

My own feeling regarding the selling of captive-bred chameleons versus wild-caught is simply that when possible it is better to purchase animals that are bred in captivity. These animals are better adjusted to living their lives in captivity by virtue of being born in a captive environment. Captive-bred chameleons are usually less stressed by parasites, shipping over long distances and are used to being housed in cages.

When buying captive-reared animals, the purchaser should go over the guidelines provided in

Figure 1.48: Captive-bred *C. verrucosus* baby.

Figure 1.49: Captive-bred baby red *C. pardalis* group shot .

Figure 1.50: *C. verrucosus* male.

this text for a prepurchase checkup and use these points to judge whether or not the animal in question is a quality lizard. Just because a chameleon is bred in captivity does not make it inherently perfect. On the contrary, many captive-bred animals are inferior to wild-caught animals because they have been reared without proper environmental and nutritional requirements.

There are only a few species of chameleons that have had enough of a gene pool established to consider them safe and without need of importations in the future. In most cases, additional importation of genetic bloodlines are needed to safely establish most species. What distresses me is the huge amount of wild-caught animals that are shipped worldwide to dealers who in turn sell them to anyone who has the money but lacks the knowledge to keep these hapless animals alive. If only there were a happy medium whereby only animals for qualified breeders and institutions would be allowed to be shipped. Alas, this is idealistic and will likely never happen in our lifetimes.

If government and private establishments would build farms for breeding chameleons within the home territories of the animals themselves, these farms would not only benefit the wild-animal populations but also the local economy. This approach is happening in Tanzania where this country has at least one farm for the breeding and export of captive-reared chameleons.

It is my opinion, that importation of vast quantities of wildlife and particularly reptiles will eventually be halted by animal rights groups, countries themselves and other pressures. It is

vital that dedicated conservationists and breeders establish these animals in self-sustaining farming operations as soon as possible and even if the market becomes flooded with captive-bred chameleons that the effort continues beyond the vagaries of the trade.

Choosing the Right Chameleons

Often we receive telephone calls from potential chameleon owners or even from experienced collectors who want to know if a particular species of chameleon will be right for them. So, our first question to them is always the same, what kind of a climatic area do they live in? If a person is going to keep a chameleon in a totally artificial environment, where the temperature and humidity will be controlled, then they need to be sure they will be able to both create and afford to sustain the animal's requirements. Alternately, if a person is counting on only modestly modifying the captive chameleon's environment, then they must find a chameleon that will like the temperature and humidity of the particular area. For example, a caller that lives in Palm Springs, California, which is a desert region known for its hot and dry summers and

Figure 1.51: Malagasy native with male *C. oustaleti*.

Figure 1.52: Male and female *C. oustaleti.*

Figure 1.53: Male *C. oustaleti.*

semi-dry winters will receive a response from us that he should try to keep the species that live in a similar native habitat and climate to his. We would recommend to this person species such as *C. verrucosus* or *C. oustaleti*, both of which will tolerate hot, dry weather and have proven to thrive in a similar climate. On the other hand if a caller lives in Seattle, Washington, then we would suggest to them that they should consider a species such as *C. quadricornis* or *C. montium* which enjoy higher humidity and lower temperatures which the climate in the Pacific Northwest of the United States provides.

We would like to see every keeper of chameleons maintain their animals outside as much as possible. The animals benefit from this treatment as well as the keepers. Animals that can be kept out of doors all summer are happier and healthier. For the collector, rearing and keeping animals outside is less maintenance.

Animals that are best suited to live in a particular climate, i.e., a desert species kept in a desert area, will survive an out-of-doors environment in that climate far better than a species that

requires an altogether different set of temperature and humidity standards. This is not to say that desert species cannot be kept by our friend in Seattle, only that he will have to make some major provisions in order to keep his desert-adapted species content. We know one very successful breeder of Jackson's chameleons, *C. jacksonii*, who lives in Tucson, Arizona, hardly a place one would think for a montane, cool-loving species. This breeder has over time acclimated his animals to accept hotter temperatures than they would normally be exposed to on Mount Kenya in Africa. This acceptance however has been mainly brought about because, along with the higher than normal temperatures, these animals are exposed to nearly 100 percent humidity level during the hot weather season. Higher humidity will cover over many ills when it comes to keeping most chameleon species in captivity. If animals kept at warmer-than-optimum temperatures can stay hydrated they can endure much warmer climates than they normally would in their native habitat.

We live in southern California in an area that receives very warm summer temperatures often exceeding 105°F. During our winter we often experience overnight freezing. We maintain a large array of chameleon species and have learned through experience that species not used to our type of climate can survive and breed when we respect their specific needs and keep them within the parameters that they experience in nature. With some species we have been able to actually push them (a bit) into an environment that is quite different from what they normally would experience in nature. I recommend to anyone trying this sort of experiment with their animals to carefully watch for signs of stress. Chameleons are generally very hardy animals if not pushed to the limits of their tolerance over and over again. It is important for chameleon keepers to be very prudent with their animals and determine exactly what the limits are for their particular species. If chameleon keepers are careful and show sensitivity for their animal's needs, they should find that it is possible to keep species with requirements other than what a backyard climate would normally provide.

Adaptability in Captivity

It is always important for the chameleon keeper to study the natural ecosystems from where their particular species have been taken, and then try to emulate these systems as closely as possible.

The biggest contributing factor to a chameleon's not doing well in captivity is that it has been placed in an inhospitable environment. Today there are hundreds of wonderful books and television programs dealing with natural science subjects on nature from around the world, giving everyone the chance to see how and where chameleons live.

It seems very obvious that one never sees plastic orchids and silk plants hanging from the trees in these animals' environments and yet many people are using these in their chameleon cages. If a living plant cannot survive inside of a chameleon's enclosure, chances are that the lizard will not fare much better! The same environmental conditions needed for the plants to thrive and grow are also necessary for the chameleon.

There are some new cage furnishings made of simulated rock that are truly beautiful and natural looking. These will help create the natural environment which is best for the animal and for the observer, and give the owner a true sense of accomplishment when they are accepted by their animal(s).

We often hear from chameleon keepers who are trying to figure out a way to water their animals more naturally and with less trouble to themselves. Somewhere out there they have heard of a ridiculous and totally unnatural method of wa-

Figure 1.55: Habitat where *C. jacksonii* are found in Hawaii.

tering their animals by placing melting ice cubes on the top of the cages. It doesn't matter where a chameleon is found in nature, whether it be the desert, mountains or tropical forest, there are no ice cubes dripping cold water for the animals to drink.

The above is an example of what not to do when trying to create a natural environment for captive animals. The correct way to present water to a chameleon would be in much the same way that they would get it in nature, namely through heavy dew (plant leaf spraying) or raindrops (sprinkling can or shower stall). The water should always be within a few degrees of what the ambient temperature is in the enclosure.

Another issue that we often see brought up concerns the correct temperature for a given animal or species. Often the keeper has a mental picture that all chameleons come from steaming jungles where the temperatures are hot and humid. Nothing could be further from the truth. In fact, a constantly hot and stuffy temperature would surely kill a chameleon as efficiently as freezing it would. Chameleons should be given every opportunity to thermoregulate themselves, like any other reptile. Chameleons should also have a fluctuation between nighttime and daytime temperatures in order to remain healthy.

The ability of healthy chameleons to adapt to life in captivity with the use of a wide range of husbandry techniques has proven to be very good. In every case I know of, the animals that are treated to an environment that is most like what they are used to in nature are the healthiest and longest lived.

Figure 1.54: Male *C. jacksonii*.

2

Choosing and Handling Pet Chameleons

Chameleons can and do make wonderful pets if the prospective keeper will follow the advice regarding the all-important environmental qualities mentioned previously. With the proper care and attention to these necessary details, these lizards can live for many years. Some of the larger species have been kept in captivity for more than 15 years. The smaller species usually live for 2–4 years.

Figure 2.1: Male *C. pardalis* captive-bred hybrid.
Photo: David Adamson

Some individual chameleons with aggressive attitudes are most likely not able or willing to be tamed. A good example of one species that usually fits this niche is the veiled chameleon, a species that only occasionally can be considered to be tamable. We have generally found this species to possess a personality that is set and unchangeable. Handling of one of these excitable lizards can cause it harmful side effects, such as upper-respiratory infections, or even lead to broken limbs if they leap off a keeper's hand. There are several species of chameleons that are better candidates as pets and are naturally tame. In this group we would include the panther, *Chamaeleo pardalis*; Parson's, *C. parsonii*; Jackson's, *C. jacksonii*; and four-horned, *C. quadricornis*, chameleons. There are many others, too numerous to mention. I do want to impress on the reader that even with the above species we have seen animals that were not at all friendly and which disdained handling. Always handle a potential pet before buying it as

Figure 2.2: Female *C. parsonii*.

Figure 2.3: Agressive female *C. pardalis*.

this will give you a better ability to choose the right animal for your needs.

The potential chameleon owner should contemplate his motive for wanting to purchase a chameleon in the first place. If the desire for wanting one of these animals is to merely own a beautiful creature or to fulfill one's ego for displaying it to friends, then certainly there are other species of lizards which are less demanding than chameleons and can accommodate these needs. Perhaps it's just the desire to have a pet as a new member of the family? Again, other species less exacting in their daily care should be considered. Chameleons are great animals but are not for everyone! Certainly after environmental factors and daily husbandry are looked at and the potential keeper's reasons for wanting one of these animals have been identified, a chameleon can be both beautiful and a satisfying pet.

Before acquiring the lizard, the best possible thing the future chameleon owner can do for both himself and his chameleon is to be prepared for its arrival. The first consideration before the animal's arrival will have to be whether a proper enclosure has been prepared for it. Next in importance would be an alternative plan if the chameleon doesn't like its new environment. Some species will not accept a walled enclosure for their environment and it will become necessary to place these chameleons on large potted indoor trees without a cage around them. Usually these animals will learn that their tree is their territory and will not wander about the home very much. In some cases when free-living animals do wander, they need their plant to be placed in a more secure location or possibly they are searching for a place to deposit eggs or are looking for water or food. It is important to remember that if a newly acquired chameleon shows signs of stress when placed in one environment, always try another approach.

Choosing a Healthy Chameleon

All prospective chameleon owners need to educate themselves with a mini-course in chameleon idiosyncrasies and illnesses before ever setting out to purchase an animal. Over and over again we have given this advice to potential buyers only to find they did not heed it and regretted it later. We often advise people to never buy a charity case from a pet store or other seller in the hope that it can be "saved." Frequently these pitiful animals are already near death, being dark and lying at the bottom of an aquarium or sitting listlessly on the edge of a bowl of water and refusing to eat or move. The buyer feels that with a little tender love and care they can pull this poor animal out of its condition. The eventual death of the lizard quite often ends up turning the new keeper against keeping chameleons forever.

Chameleons are frustratingly slow in every aspect. They catch illnesses slowly, and they regain their health with treatment even more slowly. Any healthy chameleon should be a strong, alert, eating, drinking and visually

Figure 2.4: Free-range habitats in the home.

Figure 2.5: Healthy *C. malthe* female.

Figure 2.6: Healthy *C. brevicornis* male in Madagascar.

pleasing animal. If the prospective owner will ask the following questions before purchasing any chameleon from a supplier he should be rewarded with a healthier companion animal.

1. Are the animals kept singularly? If so, how are they caged, i.e., behind glass or in screened enclosures? Do they have plenty of hiding cover?

2. How long have they been in the seller's hands? This is especially important when the seller is not familiar with proper care techniques.

3. Does the chameleon have an even, calm coloration? If the animal is exhibiting bright coloration or is almost black, is it being stressed by the presence of another animal or is this the result of an illness?

4. Are the chameleon's eyes big, bulbous or sunken? If the eyes are fused shut, is this from low humidity or from caseous matter, indicating infection.

Figure 2.7: Unhealthy male *C. pardalis* with an upper-respiratory infection.

5. Does the animal appear well hydrated? Or is its skin dry and withered looking? Does it have old dry skin hanging from its body and if so why?

6. Are the animal's shoulders, pelvis or tail thin and bony?

7. Has the seller deparasitized the animal for worms? What was the treatment and how often?

8. What does the animal's feces look and smell like? Is it runny or very odorous? If so it should be avoided.

9. Is the animal's grasp weak or strong? It should be strong for its size.

10. Are there any visible cuts, broken skin or bruises?

11. Check all four limbs to make sure they are strong and especially the feet and ankles which are often injured or even broken.

12. Are there lumps beneath the skin surface that are moveable and often elongated? These are usually filarial worms not normally effected by normal deparasitization methods.

13. If the chameleon is breathing with an open mouth, look for stringy mucus, bubbles or listen for any popping and wheezing sounds, this is usually an indication of a respiratory infection.

The above list will go a long way to providing the buyer with a checklist for selection of a healthy animal. In some cases, animals that appear perfect in every way but that have not been deparasitized can be purchased if the buyer is willing to risk the loss of the animal when asking for his veterinarian or a breeder to perform the task. We have experienced as much as a 50 percent death rate in shipments of wild-caught animals due to heavy loads of parasites being killed by treatment. These affected animals are lost from the toxicity of the dead parasites which they find difficult to expel because of the large numbers impacting the intestinal tract. For peace of mind, it is always better to buy deparasitized animals from a dealer who has taken the risk of loss and who knows what he is doing.

Today there are chameleon dealers who have caught on to the salability of deparasitized animals, but who in fact do not perform the needed treatments correctly and animals later die as a result. Make sure the person attempting to sell you a chameleon will guarantee in writing that his animals have been treated at the time of purchase. It occasionally happens that a reputable dealer will offer deparasitized animals that have received a course of deparasitization treatments only to find that the parasites have not been totally eliminated. When this happens, a reputable seller will always stand behind his animals and adjust for the error.

Handling the New Chameleon

After the chameleon has been purchased and has been brought home, the question of how to pick up the lizard properly arises.

The newly acquired animal should be approached slowly and deliberately. Place one open hand (palm up) under the front half of the animal's body and with the other hand carefully unwind the prehensile tail. Carefully push your fingers under the front feet of the chameleon making sure that it is grasping your fingers totally and lift up simultaneously. The rear feet will normally let go of the perch and will follow along.

Never yank or pull forcefully on a perched chameleon's body, legs or feet as this can cause a painful sprain or even break the ankles of an animal.

Usually a chameleon that has been handled for a while will become used to getting on the hands of its owner and the effort becomes automatic without having to pry the feet or tail loose from the perch each time the animal is handled.

Figure 2.8: Proper way to pick up a chameleon.

Figure 2.9: More of the proper way to pick up a chameleon.

3

Caring For and Housing Your Chameleon

There are probably as many theories about how to house captive chameleons as there are people keeping these animals. If we were to categorize most of these ideas, we would find that they fall into three systems for housing.

1. The first method for creating an environment ideal for captive chameleons is to allow the animal(s) semiliberty in the home by providing a small, potted tree like a *Ficus benjamina* or other hardy indoor species for the chameleon's basic living environment. These plants are not small specimens just a couple of feet tall, but rather the floor to ceiling size. Smaller versions at half the height are also acceptable for people who don't have the space. These should be placed on a small table to give them important height.

We have used the semiliberty method very successfully for keeping our Parson's chameleon colony which is normally a species that does not take well to being enclosed or housed together closely. Our Parson's roam freely in our home and each animal will generally keep to its individual tree which is stationed in every north-facing window of our living room. We enjoy the animals and the animals enjoy their liberty. Our animals feel so at home, they regularly breed and lay eggs. Each member of the colony is removed for heavy, long-term watering in the bathroom shower twice a week and on the other days we spray their plants with water from a Hudson sprayer. Fecal material is deposited by the animals every few days,

formed into a hard pellet it does not create a problem of cleanliness, most often it lands within the base of the planter where we leave it for fertilizer for the plants or is deposited in the shower stall where it is easily removed. Certainly the freedom has benefited the animals in this situation and it has made their maintenance much easier.

2. In the last few years there has been a steadily growing group of chameleon keepers who have discovered the use of enclosures that offer the animals inside of them free air exchange and that can be temperature controlled with the latest equipment specially built for that purpose. These cages are more like bird cages or aviaries with either screen or wire sides attached to a solid base where plants can be planted or eggs deposited.

Figure 3.1: Outdoor screen house enclosure in Hawaii.

Figure 3.2: Large outdoor enclosure.

These cage environments have proven themselves to be a Godsend to individuals maintaining chameleons.

In the beginning, we kept our chameleons in the same traditional glass-fronted, solid-sided cages that everyone else did and subsequently experienced all the problems associated with these kinds of enclosures. When we finally found out about the more advanced methods using screen or wire-sided cages the differences were incredible! We no longer have nearly as many mystery deaths as before and the animals live out their lives and reproduce in these habitats much as they would in nature.

Perhaps one of the most important drawbacks of the use of screen-sided cages arises from the problem of keeping a high humidity level for those species that require it. The problem is especially severe in air-conditioned rooms where the air is normally dehumidified. We have employed the use of sonic humidifiers to alleviate this problem for sensitive species and these wonderful, inexpensive machines have totally resolved the humidity problem. Combining the screen-sided cages and resultant good air flow along with the proper humidity have created an ideal habitat situation for the species that require these conditions.

There are several manufacturers making attractive, purpose-built screen or wire-sided cages for chameleons. I would advise the reader to look through the advertisements in various reptile magazines for these sources.

3. The third, and probably the most useless, method for housing chameleons is the use of solid-sided enclosures built of wood, glass, plastic, metal or a combination of these materials. Quite often the newly purchased chameleon is relegated to the imprisonment of a fish aquarium where the air quality and temperature provided is inadequate and the animal soon perishes. Other more enterprising keepers will go through the trouble to construct sizable solid-sided containers to house their animals and the results are often not any better than the fish tank. Over time these animals will tend to do poorly and unless removed and rehabilitated in a large outdoor enclosure with the proper ventilation they soon sicken and die. Chameleons are much like birds when it comes to housing them properly. Their lungs need plenty of fresh, clean air and this is almost impossible to provide in a glass tank or other solid-sided enclosure.

Another problem that we have seen all to often with glass-sided cages is that of injury to the tongue of the chameleon housed within it. These lizards do not seem to be able to recognize glass as a barrier. This often leads to them striking the glass with their tongues while trying to feed on insects that are crawling or flying nearby. The result of accidentally striking their tongues against the smooth, hard surface of the glass with such force is a bruised or sprung organ. When this happens the animal with a tongue in this condition will not be able to capture its prey in a normal manner and often will starve or pine away as a result. Sometimes these injuries are minor and the animal will regain full use of the tongue, but all too often this is not the case and animals will be lost as a result.

For some time we have wondered why animals placed in glass-fronted enclosures specially fitted with overhead lighting seem to be particularly stressed. Often the males will keep their warning coloration fired up while they are housed in this way. This causes a drain on their body reserves and they are especially affected by this type of housing. We think we have finally figured out the reason for this behavior. All one has to do is sit in a glass surrounded room with overhead lighting to quickly understand what the animal is going through. Careful observation will show that when a creature is surrounded by glass with overhead lighting a clear reflection of itself is seen in the glass. A chameleon being such a territorial and antisocial animal would be constantly on guard if it was to see its reflection all the time.

Some species of chameleons will not tolerate an enclosure of any size. It is important that the keeper recognize the symptoms of the animal's unhappiness at an early stage and remedy the situation immediately. If an individual chameleon recently placed in a new environment, i.e., cage, begins to show signs of stress such as turning black around the eyes or on the body, refusing to eat or drink, or hangs from the side or top of its cage listlessly, then it is likely that its environment is probably inappropriate for it.

If the stressed animal is given a completely new environment and it still seems listless or stressed then another problem may be causing this condition. If the keeper has not thoroughly checked his animal for internal parasites or another malady such as an upper-respiratory infection then it will be important to do so immediately. It might be necessary to obtain veterinary assistance in order to save the animal.

Anyone who has had even mild exposure to two or more chameleons at the same time will soon see that these animals are not very sociable. Experienced and successful keepers have known for a long time that keeping chameleons in their own separate enclosures works best and that these animals do not like being in close proximity to each other in a captive environment. Oftentimes animals that can even see each other from their separate enclosures can be stressed out as a result of being too close for comfort.

It is interesting to note that chameleon collectors in the field often report the closeness of animals to each other when collected. We have also seen this in our large greenhouses where colonies of species are kept in relative freedom, yet in close confinement the same chameleons that live amicably together in a much larger environment seem to despise each other. Our free-ranging Parson's chameleons living loose in our home don't seem to mind the close ranging of another Parson's. While animals kept

where they cannot get away from each other are soon stressed out and turn dark in coloration and will refuse to feed. Apparently the psychological need of being able to move out of each other's territory is very important to these animals. We always recommend to chameleon keepers that do not have a lot of room and have to keep their animals closely confined, to house their animals separately. It is necessary to make sure that the chameleons cannot see each other if it seems to stress them. This advice goes against the natural need of the human being to pair up every species possible. Chameleons are solitary creatures and it could effectively kill them if they are housed in an incorrect manner! During mating, animals kept in separate cages can be placed together under the watchful eye of the owner.

The following is a guide for appropriate enclosures at different stages in the life of captive chameleons. We have found the use of these cages invaluable for the intended purposes described below and highly recommend them to you. The breeder should understand that chameleons achieve maximum adult size only after going through several successive growth stages. Correctly constructed enclosures along with the proper placement of those containers is all important for overall success.

Outdoor Cages

Outdoor enclosures are an integral part of the overall husbandry of all chameleons in captivity. Success can be achieved for those who do not have the luxury of space for outdoor enclosures but it is hard won and demands a lot of time and work compared to the person who can keep their animals outside for part of the year. We know several remarkable breeders who raise their animals completely inside under lights, so don't become discouraged if you do not have the location necessary to try the following suggestions. I recommend (based on my own experience) that animals kept out of doors during the warmer months be given as much cage room as is possible. We have constructed aviaries for our larger species which are 12 feet long by 6 feet high by 5 feet wide. You might not enjoy the same luxury that we do for building large, aviary-style enclosures for larger animals. These species will do quite nicely in more moderate-sized pens. A size of 4–5 feet high and 3 feet wide and deep will certainly suffice. For other species, the size of the enclosures is more proportionate for the size of the animal housed within them. For instance, a medium-sized animal such as a Jackson's chameleon will be perfectly happy in a cage with the dimensions of 3–4 feet high 2 feet wide and 2 feet deep. (See Tube Cages.) In fact this size of summer cage is also good for smaller species and we try to keep to this size whenever we can. The important thing to remember here is that the cage should offer plenty of room inside for a chameleon to exercise as well as afford room for a lush plant and a couple of twisted climbing sticks or vines. Height appears to be more important than width but a minimum of 2 feet by 2 feet should be kept.

Cages should always be placed outside where the chameleons can get the benefit of the sun and have the opportunity to thermoregulate their body temperatures and get away from the direct sun if it becomes too hot.

All outdoor cages should be constructed with small-gauge hardware cloth or welded, wire fabric that will insure pest exclusion. I recommend ¼ inch by ¼ inch size as this will keep out almost any other animal that could be dangerous for a chameleon. We have known of chameleon keepers who used larger-sized mesh wire and who had losses to their lizards from rats, snakes and cats. Wire gives strength and is easily worked with by anyone. It is also important for the ventilation it provides. We use this material for the construction of our indoor cages as well. Aluminum window screening stretched over a durable frame can also be used but it is more easily torn or chewed through by vermin or other pets intent on eating the chameleons inside. The screen can also file down the chameleon's much-needed sharp toenails.

While constructing the outdoor enclosure it is important to make sure that the base and top of the cage is solid or at least strong enough to support the wire or screen sides. In the event that the cage is knocked over by children, dogs or other animals the cage should not be able to collapse on itself.

Usually we rate the size of the cage to the size of the species when it is fully grown or for its present growth stage.

Table 3.3

Adult Chameleon	Size	Mesh Size
Small	3 – 6"	¼"
Medium	7 – 12"	½"
Large	13" +	½"

If it is possible to have even larger cages, then so much the better. Cages built for rearing newly hatched or born specimens require different dimensions and construction techniques.

Size and Construction of Indoor Adult Cages

The enclosures built for housing chameleons indoors are quite similar to those needed for outdoor housing of these animals. Some differences are that the cages can be constructed with a larger size mesh of wire because the predator problems are less and the large mesh is better for visibility. The cages can be built with or without a frame depending on taste and structural strength needed for a particular location in the home. The frame-built cage will tend to withstand the abuse of time. The all-wire cage built with panels that are connected with metal, hog-type rings are functional and will give many years of service also. There are several companies that are manufacturing really beautiful and functional cages of the dimensions and standards needed for chameleons. These will be especially appreciated by the nonhandyman or the person desiring a furniture-quality look to the enclosure.

Doors in the enclosure need to be large enough for the breeder to perform regular maintenance, retrieve the chameleon or collect the eggs. The door probably can never be made too big. Many times I wish we had built our cages with larger openings for maintenance sake. It is a lot easier to replace that dying philodendron or broken perch when the door is large. In fact, a simple design incorporates the entire front or side panel as the door.

If the cage is owner built, be sure to cover or

Figure 3.3: Two indoor vivariums with screens.

Figure 3.4: Indoor vivariums with screens.

otherwise dull any exposed edges on wire surrounding the door opening. If attention was not paid to this when the cage was constructed the keeper will regret it. I can't count the times I've raked my hands and arms over rough wire when putting in or taking out an animal from an improperly built cage. It is a simple matter to

cover the rough edge of wire mesh either with liquid silicone or another piece of wood. One method a bird breeder friend suggested and that really works is to purchase clear surgical or aquarium tubing and slit it along its length then push the tubing onto the wire edge. Another good reason for covering a rough wire edge is the safety of the chameleons themselves.

Some chameleon keepers have had problems with ants which have attacked their animals within their cages. If the reader has ant problems and fears that they might attack their animals then the following might prove useful. If the cage sits on legs, put the bottom of the legs in a small container of salad oil or vinegar so ants can't get to the chameleon. If the cage does not have legs it might be advisable to attach some short ones to the bottom only a couple of inches high and follow the same method. Make sure the ants do not have another bridge to cross over into the cage. Keeping the cage free of dead insects will also keep the ants away, as that is what first attracts the ants.

Tube Cages

This is an inexpensive and very functional enclosure for most species of small to medium-sized chameleons. A good friend passed this design on to us, and we use them extensively because they are cheap, functional and can be moved with ease.

To construct one of these, simply go to a build-

Figure 3.5: Two photos of tube cages.

ers' center and purchase two 17-inch circular, plastic water pans used for catching the water under potted plants. Also obtain a piece of 4-foot tall, ¼-inch hardware cloth that is at least 54 inches long, and a tube of 100 percent pure silicone, often used for aquariums and sealing glass. Finally, buy some tie wire or plastic electric ties. Measure the 4-foot-wide wire to a running length of 54 inches and cut with wire cutters. Be sure to clip off any rough wire edges with wire clippers.

Roll the wire into a tube (using one of the 17-inch lids as a guide for circumference size) and secure along the edge with pieces of tie wire or plastic ties. Place one end of the wire tube inside one of the pans and seal the wire edge to the pan with the silicone. Place the remaining pan on the top of the tube, but do not glue with the silicone. This top pan will hold the structure secure until the silicone has fused the wire to the dish at the bottom. When the silicone has dried, place a small *Ficus benjamina* tree, about 2½–3 feet high, inside and a piece of tree branch that will extend from the bottom to the top for the animal to climb on. A shallow feeding dish about 6 inches in diameter with semi to straight edges should also be placed inside the structure. The unglued top pan will serve as an entrance. The enterprising builder can cut a door in the side if desired. Now the cage is ready to accept the chameleon. Place the unglued pan on top of the tube cage with the animal in it and viola you have a simple but effective enclosure. We recommend that you poke some small ¹⁄₁₆- to ⅛-inch holes in the top pan as this will allow water to rain on the inside of the tube cage when watering the animal with a hose or with a drip cup. The top can be secured by either placing a heavy object or potted plant on top or by using twist ties normally used for plastic bags. It is important to secure the top as we have had animals escape by pushing the top pan open. Because we sometimes have a lot of these temporary cages in use we have used small, elastic cords (bungee cords) with attached hooks for a quick and easy top fastening device.

To help assist you when moving a full tube cage, place two handles opposite each other in the wire sides. Simply use some of the tie wire to make the handles. This really helps when it comes to moving animals that need indoor-outdoor rotation.

Subadult Enclosures

Subadult chameleons generally range between the ages of 4 and 12 months, depending on the species and the rate of growth. Some chame-

Figure 3.6: Feeding dish placement inside a tube cage.

leons reach full maturity at 9–14 months, while others take as long as 24 months.

Size and Construction

Small and medium subadult animals can be housed in smaller tube cages or other enclosures made of wire or wood-and-screen. Smaller tube cages can be constructed in the same way as above except you will use 2-foot wide wire instead. It has been our experience with young and subadult chameleons that they require a constant availability of insects in order to get a good start and continue growing. For this reason we find that any enclosure housing these animals will need to be wrapped or built with a fine-mesh window screening preferably made from aluminum which the feeder insects cannot chew through. If you do use the above tube cage method for housing young or subadult animals you will need to add the screen to the tube cage before fusing it to the dish with the silicone. This can be accomplished by simply cutting the screen to the appropriate length and width of the already existing wire. Wrap the screen around the wire tube and fasten it with duct tape or large rubber bands then fuse the screen and wire simultaneously to the water dish. Lately we have found that we do not always have enough of these cages for the amount of animals that are on hand so we have had to improvise. Common nursery shade cloth of a finer mesh size wrapped tightly around an already existing tube cage has served us well excepting that some insects do manage to infiltrate through the edges.

The use of a shorter width of wire for subadult-sized chameleon cages is based on our experience while trying to raise these small creatures. We have experienced higher mortality in newborn animals up through subadult sizes when we have provided taller raising cages for them. Apparently these animals need to be very near their food source (generally pinhead crickets and fruit flies) and if they get too far away from the source of these they starve. We found that by giving them smaller enclosures and limiting the amount of young in them we have had far better luck at rearing them to adulthood.

Enclosures for Newborns

Very little differs between the enclosures described above for subadults and newborn chameleons. The main difference being that newborns can generally be kept in groups of 6–10 animals for a period of 2–4 months in a tube cage as described above. This is generally not a problem with most species when they are very young but some species such as Oustalet's chameleon, *Chamaeleo oustaleti*, seem to like living by themselves even when newborn and for these we recommend individual housing. In some species we have noted that babies kept separately from birth will grow faster and larger than those kept in groups. This seems to vary between clutches and individual animals and is not a hard and fast rule. Given the choice, we would prefer to provide separate housing for each animal as soon as is possible after birth. It

Figure 3.7: Small tube cage recommended for newborn chameleons.

goes without saying that the keeper should never mix chameleons of different ages together when there is a wide variance in size. Hatchling chameleons will be psychologically repressed when kept together with more dominant and larger animals. We have had larger animals attempt to eat smaller siblings. The animals should be separated in groups that compare in size. When any aggressive behavior is observed between siblings like biting, hissing or displaying bright coloration, it is your cue to remove the babies to separate enclosures that will give them both privacy and safety.

Newborn chameleons need a constant supply of live insects for food. These small lizards have tongue lengths in proportion to their body sizes and should be provided with accommodations that are proportionally smaller in the beginning. This can be accomplished by scaling down the size of the enclosure to keep food within constant reach.

Enclosures for Gravid Females

Noticeably gravid female chameleons should be housed by themselves in an enclosure that offers them seclusion and security. A gravid female that is not provided with these amenities will constantly be searching for another location and will retain her eggs or babies for too long a time period. In captivity, it is a simple thing to give these lizards the proper habitat for egg laying or giving birth with a minimum of trouble.

Figure 3.9: Female *C. parsonii* laying eggs.

Figure 3.8: Female *C. parsonii* in a trash can depository.

If I could always have my way, I would like to have gravid female chameleons deposit their eggs in the same enclosures that they permanently live in. These eggs could then be removed to a safer incubation area after being buried by the female. It is stressful for a female to be removed from her normal territory and then be placed in a depository (an egg-laying or birthing enclosure discussed below) area.

This said, I must concede that time and again out of necessity we have had to place our females in more appropriate depository cages where they have laid their eggs without any apparent problems.

When a gravid female is ready to lay her eggs there are several important factors that should be in place to ensure success. The enclosure that she is in must be clean and have good ventilation. We provide a base that can hold at least twelve inches of good quality potting soil for her to dig and lay her eggs in. We also provide a plant such as *Ficus benjamina* for her to climb and rest on.

Extremely important to the egg-laying female is the depth of the media in which she will lay her eggs this should exceed at least the length of the female's body. If possible, the laying media should be at a depth of twice the length of the nesting female, in order for her to feel secure before laying her eggs.

Proper moisture content of the substrate in which the eggs will be deposited is also a very important factor for success. After placing at least twelve inches of potting soil in the bottom of the enclosure, we begin adding water a little at a time, thoroughly mixing it. Enough water is added to allow the potting soil to become quite damp but not soggy. When the soil is squeezed tightly in the fist and then released, it should bind together without falling apart. At this consistency it should be quite acceptable to the female for egg laying purposes. It is important that the soil will bind together well enough that it will not collapse in on the tunneling female at the time of egg laying. If the soil is left too wet in the depository, the female will likely not lay her eggs there or if she does they will most certainly drown.

After experimenting with a wide assortment of cages and other containers in which to construct a proper egg depository we have come to the conclusion that a simple thirty-gallon plastic garbage can best fits our needs for this purpose. They are widely available, cheap and will allow for security and seclusion to the female chameleon. They do not need to be covered over as the animal cannot escape unless given a plant or branches that are too tall. The bottom is waterproof and will hold a good depth of potting soil for egg deposition.

Although at first we felt that the trash cans might be too closed in and cause sensory deprivation to the female chameleons, they have in fact surprised us, as most females really seem to like these containers for egg-laying purposes.

Figure 3.10: *C. parsonii* eggs unearthed.

Ideally, a normal enclosure housing the female can be rigged to serve as a depository cage when the time for egg laying comes. The beauty of such a cage allows the female to live in her home territory and merely go to the bottom of that enclosure and deposit her eggs when the time arrives, without much disturbance or stress. Construction of such a cage is fairly easy for the handyman and can be made to be simple but attractive, which is more than can be said of the trash can depository. The cage should be constructed to the correct dimensions to house the particular species in question. A suggestion would be 4 feet tall by 2 feet square for small and medium-sized animals. Instead of having a solid bottom in the cage an actual false bottom area is built. This will allow a media-filled container to be placed underneath for the female to dig in. When the female has completed covering her eggs, the container can be removed with little disturbance, and the top floor can be replaced for normal maintenance.

Foliage

Plants and chameleons go together like spots and leopards. Only in the rarest instances could one see a chameleon in nature far from the cover of a bush or tree. In captivity, living plants with good, dense leaf cover are essential to the environment of a chameleon.

We have experimented with several species of indoor plants that are commonly grown into small trees in order to see which ones work well in the cages of chameleons. Without a doubt the best species that we have found so far is the Benjamin fig, *Ficus benjamina*. It is nontoxic and very hardy. It can take the abuse of a lizard climbing on it and adjusts well to low light intensities. The leaves are eaten by very few insects but are enjoyed by the veiled chameleon, *C. calyptratus*, which eats it with gusto!

There are many other species of plants that can also serve the same purpose if *Ficus benjamina* does not suit your tastes. House plant books can be found at your local library. Garden centers are usually good places to search out treelike species suitable for culture inside the home.

It is important to remember not to buy plants that could be toxic to your animals in any way as at least one species of chameleon eats plant material. Secondly and even more important is the fact that feeder insects that are not eaten by a chameleon right away will feed on the plants in the enclosure and if any of these are toxic they may not affect the insect but could kill the chameleon feeding on them. There are many species of houseplants that are toxic and it is important to research the subject well before purchasing any of these.

Watering or Hydration

Chameleons, without exception, should get the chance to drink water for body hydration at least once a day. Some species will partake of water whenever it is offered, others will not.

Chameleons exposed to higher atmospheric humidity levels will not require the same amount of water as animals kept in a drier environment. Chameleons receive a lot of their body fluids from breathing in humid, moisture-laden air and this acts to keep them hydrated in nature even when it hasn't rained for sometime. During the dry season, chameleons subsist solely on the night and early morning air which is still quite laden with moisture.

Newborn, captive chameleons should be offered water as fine droplets at least twice a day and preferably more often then this. Young animals will dehydrate at an alarming rate if not kept fully hydrated at all times. In nature these smaller chameleons are usually found around the most humid areas possible.

If the keeper neglects watering his chameleons for longer then a few days and his animals do not have high humidity levels within their enclosures they will quite likely develop severe kidney problems that are often irreversible.

Proper hydration is very easy to accomplish by means of using a simple hand-held garden sprayer or as complex as automatic watering devices connected to time clocks that take away the worry of watering these animals during the

Figure 3.11: Mister inside a small tube cage.

owner's absence. The important thing is to have a system that will rain water onto the chameleons for a period of at least fifteen minutes, preferably longer, until they are satiated.

Merely spraying a fine mist over some leaves and a chameleon's body with a hand-held atomizer once a day is not proper hydration! We often see chameleon keepers use these hand-held atomizers spraying away at their animals for a few brief seconds and often blasting away at the chameleons face with a steady stream of water that causes the animal to shut its eyes and try to retreat. This obviously is not a proper hydration technique! In nature chameleons drink from heavy morning dew or rain drops that fall on them and nearby surfaces that they can lick. Normally these drinking periods last for a half an hour or longer and it is remarkable to see just how much water one of these animals can consume at one time. Usually the action of

falling raindrops triggers the drinking response in chameleons almost immediately.

A fairly simple and inexpensive watering system for captive animals can be made from utilizing drip line tubing made for watering plants. These uncomplicated systems can be designed to water either one animal or a whole collection. There are literally hundreds of different attachments for these systems. Some can create a fine mist spray and others can be made to emulate rain drops. We find the latter to be the best for watering animals and the fine mist head being more useful for lowering high temperatures in the area. Obviously this particular system needs to be used for outdoors applications or in a greenhouse situation.

If the keeper cannot house his animals in a place where the water runoff is not a problem then another simple system can be used that is functional and inexpensive. Simply take a quart-sized Styrofoam cup used for holding soup or other bulky liquids and put a small pin-sized hole in the bottom of it. Fill with water that is approximately the same temperature as the air surrounding the chameleon. Do not make the mistake of making the hole too large so that a lot of water will run out of the cup all at once. You will be able to gauge the amount of flow by the size of the hole and it might require some practice to get it just right. The idea is to allow a steady dripping effect from the bottom of the cup when placed in or on top of the cage. A corresponding catch basin can be placed on the bottom of the cage to collect any runoff. The water should cascade through the leaves slowly enough to allow the chameleon to drink the amount it needs over a period of time. With any mechanical watering system it is sometimes necessary to make the animal in the enclosure aware that water is available, this is done by first spraying it with an atomizer for a few seconds prior to starting the dripping from the watering cup.

Some commercially made drip-drinking devices have recently entered the pet market. These drip bottles are filled up and then allowed to slowly drip down through the top of the cage in the same manner as the drip cup mentioned above.

The reader should be cautioned at this point that

Figure 3.12: Drip cup atop a tube cage.

these drip-type watering units can prove to be dangerous to chameleons if not properly used and like any commercial or homemade product the user must understand the concept behind them before use. Rain forest species sometimes cannot use this system because they do not recognize the dripping water as a drinking source and became severely dehydrated. Sometimes it is possible to remedy this problem by just changing the drip rate of the drops or by adjusting the plant that the water is dripping through. The important thing to remember is that the animals exposed to these mechanical drinkers must be monitored closely. A chameleon that never has to search for water to drink is more likely to thrive in captivity with a lower level of stress. The keeper might assume that because he has seen the animal drink one time from one of these systems that the animal will automatically use it every time it needs water, this is not necessarily so. Many chameleon keepers live very busy lives and have tight schedules so out of necessity they try to cut corners with the care of their animals. These drip drinkers are viewed as a device to assist them in their busy lives. What

happens so often is that the keeper becomes lazy and does not pay proper attention to the use of one of these water containers and doesn't notice that it has for some reason become plugged or has become mineralized and is only dripping very slowly and ineffectively. Don't get lazy and cause yourself the grief of losing a precious animal because you didn't monitor your drinking device!

Another important thing to note is that chameleons often drink their water over a long period of time and require that drip systems supply this water for a long enough period of time for them to become fully hydrated. Too often a drip cup or other device cannot perform their function for long enough and the animals won't receive sufficient water. Often they will not begin drinking until shortly before the water container is nearly empty. Be careful!

One system that works quite well for us is the use of a hand-held garden sprayer often referred to as a Hudson sprayer. These pressure tank sprayers will hold a considerable amount of water and can be quite effective. The only fault we find with their use is that the keeper has to stand around operating the sprayer for the duration of the animal's drinking time, when other things could be done.

Our favorite watering system for chameleons involves either putting the animals under an outdoor mist/sprinkling system used for lawns and shrubs and running tepid water through it from the sink or putting a group of compatible animals under the shower head in the bathroom. The latter is really effective in hydrating animals quickly without having to stand around while the chameleons are drinking. We have one shower stall in our home that has been donated solely for watering our chameleons. We place sturdy branches and several 3-foot specimens of *Ficus benjamina* in the stall and the animals being watered that day. The water pressure is adjusted so that it gently rains on the animals below without high pressure. I always make doubly sure that the water temperature is correct after running the water for a few seconds. Once in a while for some reason or another I will find that the water temperature dial has been readjusted and the water temperature would have scalded our animals if I had not checked it beforehand.

Some animals will need to drink water every day while others will require water every other day. For this reason we water every animal every day with a hand-held sprayer or with a garden sprinkler over their cage. Animals kept exclusively indoors are given daily watering by spraying the plant leaves in the area that they inhabit. Twice weekly we place these animals in the shower for a longer soaking. When temperatures are higher and the atmospheric humidity is low a chameleon will transpire more body fluids and will need to be watched more carefully for symptoms of dehydration. If an animal appears to be lethargic or when it is drinking it has a heavy syruplike drool from its mouth, it is most likely dehydrated and will have to be given more water more frequently.

The skin of chameleons seems to be quite porous and these animals lose substantial amounts of body fluids through it over the course of a dry day. In really hot weather an increase in humidity around the lizards will help them maintain their body fluids more easily. This is especially true for those species that normally do not become exposed to high temperatures in nature such as Jackson's, *C. jacksonii*; four-horned, *C. quadricornis*; Parson's, *C. parsoni*; and other montane rain forest species. This type of hydration is also the only way available for a chameleon to wash its eyes thereby reducing the chances of eye infections. During long-term hydration, the chameleon will absorb water through the skin, nose and eyes as well as drinking orally for a full body hydration.

Feeding Dishes

Quite often chameleon keepers will have problems with newly imported animals that seem to be in a stupor and are unwilling to feed on insects that are not concentrated in a small area. In other situations we have seen animals that will not cope well with insects crawling throughout their enclosure. These free-ranging insects will annoy the chameleons to the point that they will no longer feed while living within that particular cage. Over time we have adopted the practice of placing live foods in straight

sided but shallow plastic containers that do not allow the insects to escape easily from them. In this way we can monitor the feeding habits of the individual chameleons in whose cages we place these dishes and avoid problems with free-roving insects. Crickets in particular will eat the feces of chameleons and if these happen to be newly imported animals that haven't been deparasitized, these insects could become the vector for spreading parasites to other animals that have been already treated. We really try to limit the escape of crickets from one enclosure to the other for this reason. Chameleons are intelligent animals and will soon learn to recognize a feeding dish as a place to find food. For this reason we place feeding dishes at levels that the animals prefer to feed. It is important to place climbing perches near the top surfaces or directly over feeding dishes so the animals have access to them.

A number of feeding station containers can be utilized that are practically inescapable for in-

Figure 3.13: Male *C. oustaleti* eating out of a food bin.

Figure 3.14: Another shot of a male *C. oustaleti* eating out of a food bin.

sects and that are accessible to the chameleons. We are currently using the smallest sizes of small, plastic, animal enclosures sold by pet shops for carrying mice or small reptiles. By removing the small top door and both handles and placing two plastic-coated electric wires about eight inches to a foot long in their place, we are able to hang these stations on limbs or vines below the areas where the chameleons are. The chameleons will soon learn to use these plastic boxes with great efficiency.

Everything written above regarding feeding dishes applies to semi-adult and adult animals only. We find it is nearly impossible to offer pinhead-sized crickets and fruit flies in a feeding dish to newborn chameleons. In the case of these animals, keepers will have to suffer through the ordeal of escaped fruit flies and pinhead crickets joining them for dinner.

Occasionally some animals will be very stubborn about feeding from a particular dish and adjustments will have to be made. Sometimes this will involve changing to a more open-topped container or one made of a different material. We do not recommend the use of glass containers of any kind however, as we have experienced a problem with glass bruising the hard, striking tongues of chameleons. Hard plastic dishes do not seem to cause this same health problem and we use these instead. These plastic feeding dishes or boxes also offer the keeper an added convenience as well, because they enable the collector the ability to keep mineral- and vitamin-dusted insects in a small area so that they will not disperse their nutrient coatings onto plants and other surfaces in the enclo-

Figure 3.15: Female *C. oustaleti* eating out of a feeding bin.

sure before being consumed by the chameleons.

If a chameleon does refuse to eat from a particular feeding station then the only other choice is to try hand feeding the animal by holding up live insects with the fingers close to the animal's face (10 inches) or allowing free-ranging insects for limited time periods until the chameleon can be trained to eat from a station which usually happens fairly quickly if the owner has the patience to work with the animal, however this shouldn't be done with neonates. Some animals will be very shy and will not eat in the presence of the keeper. These animals should be placed in a quiet area away from traffic and watched from several yards away to make sure they are eating. Often with these animals we will place crickets or other insects on their climbing branches before backing away from them.

Force feeding a chameleon should always be a last resort for the keeper. We have seen certain instances when it was necessary and it saved an animal's life. In most cases it had the opposite effect and stressed the stubborn animal to the point that it died.

Highways and Byways

Anyone who has kept pet birds in a cage usually knows that it is important to alter the circumference and shapes of their perches in order to promote good circulatory function to the feet. This same husbandry rule applies for chameleons who surprisingly enough, have feet very much like those of birds. Climbing perches should consist of tree or shrub branches that are pliable and have different circumferences. We like to use old grapevines (trailing trellis or creepertypes like Concord or Thompson seedless varieties) which keep their shape well and are flexible after drying and vary circumference size over their length. These vines can be used to make "highways in the skies" so to speak and can create a really nice effect for your animals to climb about the cage or the house if you so choose.

If a chameleon is allowed to only climb on hard, uniform-sized perches such as dowels, etc., it will eventually develop foot problems such as hard calluses on the foot pad, sores and stiff

Figure 3.16: Red *C. pardalis* in a stick structure.

arthritic joints in its toes. Chameleons should get every opportunity to exercise their feet on soft springy surfaces such as fresh green branches, vines or as a last resort on soft cotton ropes that cannot unravel easily and entangle the animals' feet or tail.

Natural Sunlight

Natural sunlight is as important to a chameleon as water is to a fish. Without its beneficial rays these reptiles will not grow and develop normally. Chameleons deprived of natural sunlight may survive in captivity and even reproduce for a generation or two without its benefits but they will never be all that they can be without its life-giving benefits. Modern day science has attempted to duplicate the benefits of the sun's rays by developing special lights that emit various spectral qualities. Some of these lamps have been shown to benefit reptiles and other animals under captive conditions and are far superior to the often-used common incandescent bulbs. We have experimented with some of the modern, so-called reptile lamps and have seen real benefits from them for chameleons that could not be

exposed to regular sunlight for one reason or another. Nevertheless we also keep chameleons that are regularly exposed to unfiltered natural sunlight and there is no comparison between the health and vitality of animals exposed to this treatment and those under artificial lamps. Recently a European journal reported that even at their best, artificial fluorescent lights can barely approach the quality of natural sunlight and its effects. One of these artificial lights can only approximate $\frac{1}{150}^{th}$ the intensity of sunlight

Common problems with animals that are exposed only to synthetic sunlight bulbs include metabolic bone disease, edemas of the throat and limbs, egg-bound females, digestive problems, upper-respiratory and skin infections. These problems can be caused from other factors as well (see Chameleon Health). Some keepers include the use of special ultraviolet lights along with these special fluorescent bulbs. I cannot comment on the use of these lights as I have not used them, but some breeders feel they are beneficial and that they have helped their animals much more than the use of the reptile bulbs alone.

If the enclosures of chameleons can only be kept outside for short periods of time it is essential to place them where the animals can bask for at least an hour a day. If this is impossible for the owner, weekend basking is still better than none at all.

A little direct sunlight goes a long way, but constant direct sunshine beating down on an animal's enclosure will prove to be too hot and will soon cook it. Some species of chameleons do not seem to withstand much direct sunlight at all. We have observed species with a noticeable aversion to sunlight that will try to escape from it as if it were burning them. Species such as Parson's chameleon, *Brookesia* and other deep-forest species are in this group. Even with these species, the animals like to warm themselves in the early morning with the fresh but cooler rays of the sun. This warming allows them to become more active during the morning hours when food is more available and they will be able to catch and digest it more efficiently. With adults as well as young chameleons, discretion is necessary when placing their cages into a sunny location. A shady location broken with sunny patches is the most ideal location for placing the cage. This location should be watched over and checked frequently because as the sun moves throughout the day, the cage can become too exposed to the direct rays and they will kill animals, especially young chameleons. Ideally, the perfect spot for a cage would allow some sunlight and shade on a full-time basis. One of the distinct advantages of large outdoor aviaries for chameleons is their ability to more easily provide shady and sunlit areas for the animals.

Figure 3.17: Female *C. pardalis*—blue morph in blanched coloration due to heat stress.

When keeping chameleon enclosures inside, place them in a northern exposure or if living in the Southern Hemisphere in a southern exposure. Never place the chameleon enclosure directly in the sun behind a glass window, as the animal can very quickly become overheated from the sun shining through the glass which magnifies its intensity. If an enclosure contains glass sides, do not set it in the direct sun, as this can literally cook the chameleon within minutes.

Cleanliness

Keeping a chameleon's environment clean is essential to its long-term health. The transfer of many potentially dangerous diseases is primarily passed to a chameleon due to keeper negligence. The use of disinfectant products such Shaklee's Basic G as a germicide or common household bleach will reduce the passing of many infections caused from often pathogenic bacteria. It is important to note here that almost all disinfectants on the market have very little effect on parasites and particularly their eggs. This is why it is so important to deparasitize animals in a quarantine area away from other already-clean individuals. Any surfaces subject to contact of fecal materials from infected specimens should be thoroughly wiped with disposable paper towels and then disinfected with a broad-spectrum disinfectant immediately. Even the use of latex gloves while cleaning possibly infected animals is warranted for the collector's health sake! Use all disinfectants with caution and as directed and be sure to remove your animal from the close proximity of their use as chameleons are quite sensitive to fumes from these products. Mixing ammonia and household bleach will create toxic fumes so quickly that the keeper will have to rush out of the area and leave animals behind, so never mix these two or any other cleaning agents together unless the labels make allowances for this.

Always consider a cage used by another species of reptile or chameleon to be potentially contaminated by pathogens or possibly with parasite ova. Never place new or long-term specimens into a previously used enclosure without disinfecting it completely beforehand. This advice is sometimes hard to follow and an emergency situation will arise when it is tempting to use a previously used enclosure without disinfecting it first. This won't usually cause a problem, but when it does it can be devastating and hard on one's conscience.

Cleaning the enclosure on a weekly basis will reduce the potential of attracting lethal pests such as ants that can attack and kill live chameleons. We know of more than one instance where these insects have had truly disastrous effects on a whole collection.

As much as cleanliness is important to keeping these animals, it is also important to the keeper's health. Chameleons, as well as other reptiles, can carry bacteria and possibly parasites that potentially could also be harmful to humans, it should become an automatic habit to wash your hands thoroughly with soap and water after handling these animals.

4

Feeding Chameleons

It is a natural tendency for a new chameleon owner to want to get their chameleon to eat. After all, considering all the bizarre things chameleons do, capturing their food with a sure-shot tongue is certainly one of the most fascinating. It's only after the animal refuses to feed on the first try that the new owner becomes alarmed and usually seeks help from others with some experience. We often receive frantic telephone calls from concerned new owners who are afraid their animals are starving to death. Usually we find that the animal has not been given enough time to acclimate to its new surroundings before it is expected to turn into a three-ring circus performer.

Most new keepers are surprised to discover that unless the animal is very emaciated it can survive for many days without eating. Far more important than eating is the hydration of the new arrival. Usually a well-hydrated animal will begin feeding soon after it has arrived.

It is always a good practice to begin offering food to a new animal with as wide a choice of species of insects as is possible to obtain. Some animals will not recognize a mealworm or a cricket as food and may need to be coaxed into eating this more "normal" fare over a period of time. We know of animals that would only eat snails or grasshoppers when they first arrived. It is a rare animal that will refuse a juicy black cricket or grasshopper soon after they become settled into captivity and few chameleons can refuse a housefly.

After a chameleon becomes acclimated to life in captivity it will normally accept whatever kinds of insects it is offered. There are exceptions of course and some animals will favor certain species of insects over others. Many times an animal will eat only giant mealworms for several weeks and then all of a sudden they will no longer regard the mealworms as food. This can also happen with other insect species. In this case, changing to a new species of insect or a variety of insects will usually do the trick and the chameleon will resume feeding. Feeder-insect burnout is a fairly frequent result of animals being fed on a single type of insect over a period of time without being offered other species from time to time. Burnout rejection of a particular food item is probably a natural response to ensure that a chameleon will receive as wide a nutritional balance of vitamins and minerals as possible. These nutritional components in an animal's diet are necessary to maintain its health and well being over its lifetime. By feeding a captive chameleon only one or two species of insects the owner predisposes his animal to a shorter life span and ill health. We do know of animals that have never had feeder-insect burnout and only eat giant mealworms and have done so for years. The animals appear to be healthy and do reproduce. The key to their doing so well on such an apparently unbalanced diet is that the insects they do eat are nutritionally gut loaded and dusted with proper nutrients, which enables their keeper to get proper nutrition into them. We favor the greatest variety approach for our own animals and try to offer at least three different types of insects on a daily basis. It is usually not too difficult to train stubborn animals to eat a variety of insects if you are persistent and have the time to work with them.

Because chameleons come from so many divergent habitats in nature, they are accustomed to certain species of insects more than others. It appears from what we have observed in Hawaii with Jackson's chameleons, and from what other friends have reported to us from Africa and Madagascar, that the backbone of most chameleons' diets is mainly based upon various species of flies. Nutritional studies of domestically raised houseflies show them to be deficient in a number of nutrients. Houseflies are sufficient in proteins and some vitamins but lack many other especially important minerals. When these deficient insects are nutrient loaded by either feeding them on enriched diets or dusting with specific ingredients, they become an excellent food choice for a wide range of reptile and amphibian species. Other species of insects such as crickets and mealworms are likewise deficient in all important minerals such as calcium, magnesium and trace micronutrients and can be enhanced through the use of specifically prepared foods and by dusting with powders made for this purpose.

Some people will not use wild-collected insects for feeding to their reptiles. They feel that these insects are potential carriers of parasites. They are correct. We do offer our animals wild-collected insects for the nutritional balance that they offer and we do not regret this at all. Periodical checking for parasites has demonstrated that the danger of picking up our native species of parasites is quite small and we have rarely found them to be a problem in our own chameleons. We do find an occasional roundworm egg in our previously deparasitized animals and when discovered, we treat with a parasite-specific medication. We are not at all sure that the occasional worm eggs we experience are even derived from the native wild insects that we occasionally feed. These might be holdovers from the original parasite load that arrived with these animals in the first place. It is not unusual to find that even after repeated worming with the proper drug that some parasites have not been totally eliminated. Out of necessity we

mainly have to use insects that are domestically produced because of the numbers of animals that we maintain. The occasional use of a wild-caught insect from an unpolluted area will do your animal far more good than harm and offers important variety that, even for chameleons, is the spice of life. We would like to see a much wider assortment of insect species on the market and perhaps demand will finally cause this to happen.

Chameleons will often overeat when given the opportunity and this is unhealthy and dangerous for them. In nature, these animals will take every opportunity to eat when it presents itself. Most species have to be constantly alert for an insect meal and expend a great deal of time and energy hunting for it.

One often sees documentary films that show chameleons sitting around waiting for their food to come to them. This gives the impression that these animals are sedentary and not willing to work for their food. This is not at all accurate as we often observe hungry animals wandering about looking for food. When they are fed what they need they then languish around until their meal is digested then are on the prowl again for more food. It is not healthy for a chameleon to eat 10–20 fully grown crickets or other insects of comparable size a day. Usually 3–5 insects of the correct size for the size of the animal being fed, are more than sufficient for an adult chameleon that is in good physical condition. We will offer an animal the size of an adult panther chameleon, *Chamaeleo pardalis*, 5–6 full-grown brown crickets or 2 of the larger black crickets, a couple of giant mealworms or perhaps a tomato hornworm during one feeding and only twice a week at the most. On some days we may offer only a half-dozen giant mealworms and the next feeding, three large grasshoppers. There is not a set amount of food that is necessary only that it is not given to the extent that the animals become obese and lethargic most of the time. It is important that the chameleon becomes active and hunts for its food between meals. Most species will grow restless when they become hungry and this is the keeper's signal to provide a good meal to the chameleon.

Always offer live, healthy insects that are fed on proper, natural foodstuffs or specially prepared nutrients for gutloading. Insects being fed only on branmeal and a carrot which is usually the case, are nutritionally deficient and will not pass much-needed nutrients on to the feeding chameleon. Likewise, insects fed on poultry meals such as Layeena do provide more nutrition but are also loaded with synthetic vitamins that are now coming under fire from scientists and chameleon keepers alike, as they are a suspected cause of health problems in chameleons and other reptiles. The laying hen preparations are intended to provide a chicken with what it needs for its short 3-year life span before it goes to the soup maker. In addition to having the wrong form of vitamins, these feeds also are very high in phosphates that counteract the level of calcium and this is clearly not needed in the captive management of chameleons. It is the phosphorous that is already overabundant in the insect's body that makes it necessary for the chameleon keeper to add additional calcium to the insects being fed. The last thing a feeder insect needs to be eating is food with even more phosphorous in it.

We are seeing problems with gout and edema in several species of chameleons that are receiving vitamin A in its synthetic form either directly or through feeder insects. Often a caller will say that they are not feeding anything with synthetic vitamin A in it yet their animals are getting edema. The mistake they are making though is that they are not allowing their newly purchased feeder insects a long enough time to clean their intestinal tract out before feeding them to their chameleons. The companies that raise feeder insects commonly use poultry or other feeds that have synthetic vitamins as a component. These are passed on to the lizards unless they are allowed at least three days after arrival to purge themselves of this material. If you cannot feed your insects on foods purposely developed without synthetic vitamins then it is vital to supply them with foodstuffs that are nutritionally balanced with minerals and vitamins but are natural in form. We do not feed insects to animals that are not prefed a wide assortment of vegetables and some fruits first. We recommend that at least 3 days pass before

Figure 4.1: One of the many stick insects in Madagascar.

feeding newly acquired insects to your chameleons. During these 3 days feed the insects on deep green vegetables such as broccoli, squash and kale. We also feed apples and oranges as a moisture source to the insects. Shortly before feeding to the chameleons we gutload and dust with minerals all of the insects that are going to be given to our animals.

One bit of advice to those who consider feeding pinkie mice to their chameleons—Don't! Mice are rarely, if ever, a part of a chameleon's natural diet and require digestive enzymes that a chameleon does not possess in order to digest them properly. Mice also harbor bacteria in their guts that are not normally found in a healthy chameleon and these can cause intestinal upset. Large chameleons will sometimes take pink mice but will not thrive on them. We have known people who have tried the lazy way out by trying to maintain their chameleons on soaked dog food fed by hand. Neither the chameleons nor the would-be keepers are still around. Feed these lizards the foods they have eaten over the eons of time—insects!

It is seldom advisable to force feed a chameleon that isn't eating. This practice is not only very stressful for them but also is rarely of any benefit. It is far more important to find out what the cause of the problem is that is preventing the animal from eating. The problem could be physical or psychological in nature and should be researched and remedied as quickly as possible. When a chameleon is sick, it doesn't feel like eating anymore than a sick human feels like eating. During times of inappetence it is very important to make sure that the animal is not dehydrating and it is essential that the chameleon be kept humid and watered during this time. Even critically sick chameleons will usually drink water.

During the cooler winter months, chameleons that are kept cool (not cold) may only eat an occasional insect in a week's time. This is natural and should not cause alarm. Because they are cold-blooded their entire metabolism slows down with the cooler weather and having food that is not being digested in their stomachs and intestines will cause them problems. During this time it is essential to offer a basking spot that provides some heat for digestion of food during the daytime. This is easily done by placing one of the reptile basking lights over a spot frequented by the animal. Make certain to use the correct receptacle for the light as the light can get very hot and can cause a fire or meltdown. Also make sure the animal cannot touch the appliance in any way or it could suffer from burns. Even with the aid of a basking spot chameleons usually will slow down with their appetites during the cooler times of the year. As soon as the weather warms up again they should resume eating with a vengeance and will regain body fats lost during cooler periods. Some species will not do well being cooled during some parts of the year and this should not be forced upon them. Generally these species are all from tropical areas where the temperatures usually do not go below the upper sixties Fahrenheit even at night. Check to see where the species that you keep are from and if they are not montane or desert species then it is usually a sure bet that they should not be given too much cooling during the wintertime.

Insects for Feeding

Over the years, chameleon aficionados have tested a wide assortment of available insects as potential food for chameleons. As time goes by, more and more species of insects have been added to the list of species that are excellent feeder items in the diets of these lizards. Many more varieties will become available for the trade in the near future, as demand increases for more variety. In the past, most of the feeder insects that were available to reptile keepers have come as a result of the huge business in live fish bait but now as more insects are being

Figure 4.2: Vietnamese walking stick.

Figure 4.3: Egg casing of praying mantis.

Figure 4.4: Praying mantis.   *Photo: David Adamson*

bred for feeding other animals, the live food business has expanded in scope.

Insect breeders must comply with stringent agricultural laws designed to eliminate the threat of spreading pests. Many of the insects in trade now are considered agricultural pests that are so widespread that they are ubiquitous and are not excluded from one state to the next. Introduction of possible new species to the trade requires endless hours of investigation, patience and disappointment after having applications

Figure 4.5: Tomato horn worm.   *Photo: David Adamson*

denied. In many cases, insects with great potential for feeding other animals are rejected by the authorities on grounds that their escape would pose an important agricultural threat. Some states are more restrictive than others on interstate shipments with California, Florida and Texas being the most restrictive because of the pest potential.

Many serious breeders have either tried or are currently trying to breed their own supply of insects for feeding to their animals. In most cases, these attempts fail as the culture of insects is both time consuming and needs real focus to be successful. Many species can be bred on a small supplemental basis and certainly can help with the feed bill. It is a much different situation however when it comes to raising insects on a larger scale as all of the problems with this kind of culture are magnified along with the numbers raised. Diseases and parasites often can wipe out an insect culture overnight and the facilities for rearing them on a commercial basis can be very costly to construct as well as maintain. One acquaintance of ours breeds insects for the trade and has invested well over a hundred thousand dollars in the project without seeing a profit yet.

Because a varied diet offers the soundest way to good nutrition for any animal including humans it is very important to see to it that your animals receive this consideration. It is amazing to see the difference in behavioral attitude with a chameleon that has been eating a boring diet of mealworms or crickets and suddenly has grasshoppers and lab-raised tomato hornworms added to its menu. Sometimes this is all that is required to bring an animal out of the doldrums.

I cannot stress enough that a varied diet is one of the foremost factors in promoting the health and well-being of a healthy chameleon. To give some idea of the variety of insects that have been tried on chameleons and are accepted the following list is provided. This list is by no means complete and there are virtually hundreds of other species of insects that could be bred as feeders but are not.

Butterworms or Tebo Worms

These grublike larvae are a byproduct of the fishing bait business. Butterworms are wild harvested in South America from certain species of plants in which they burrow and eat the inner lining of the stems. From the time that they are removed from these plant stems for commerce and shipped overseas, they are not fed anything for nutrition as they only specifically eat the particular species of plant from which are harvested. After harvesting, these worms live solely off their own body stores of fat and are usually shipped to the customer in sawdust that offers nothing nutritional to the insects. Butterworms are eaten eagerly by some lizards and not by others. There have been reports of digestive upset in some species that have eaten them and actual regurgitation by others. I recommend that these worms be fed sparingly as they are highly fattening to the liver. Because of their starved condition when they arrive, they should be dusted with nutrients before offered to any animals as food.

Cockroaches

Cockroaches are among the most familiar insects to readers, besides the housefly. These widespread insects are found virtually throughout the world and are usually hated by almost everybody that comes into contact with them. Cockroaches are nevertheless a very good source of nutrition to most insect-feeding animals. In addition to being nutritious, roaches offer variety from the ubiquitous brown cricket. Roaches are generally not commercially raised as food and starter cultures would have to be purchased by those keepers who feel the need to use them. Nutritionally they are identical to most wild orthopteran insects such as crickets and grasshoppers. Cockroaches are sometimes vectors of certain parasites that cannot be elimi-

Figure 4.6: Madagascar hissing cockroaches.

nated from animals once contracted, and only roaches from laboratory strains should be considered for feeding. Some chameleons seem to really recognize cockroaches as food. Our Parson's chameleons will practically kill for a nice, fat Madagascar hissing roach, they really seem to enjoy them as a treat.

There are roach species that cannot climb and escape from smooth-sided enclosures and are quite easily raised in plastic or glass containers. One species we have tried is the Central American orange-headed cockroach, *Eublaberus posticus*, which is an excellent species as a feeder insect. This species is easily reared and does not climb the walls of its enclosure and moves slowly. It can be raised in colonies and feeds on virtually any foodstuff such as dog food, fruit, vegetables, etc. This species takes awhile to become established and build up its numbers to allow for harvesting as food for animals but once this is accomplished these insects will add variety and nutrition.

Many species of roaches can climb any smooth surface and will escape with the greatest of ease. Some of these species have the potential to become pests in the home and should be avoided. Always question the raiser of these insects about their habits such as climbing ability, odor and breeding potential outside of an artificial environment. Many of the tropical roaches cannot establish themselves in the home because of certain needs that if not provided will result in their being unable to reproduce themselves. Temperature seems to be an important factor, with many species unable to reproduce at temperatures lower than 80°F.

Europeans, more than anyone else, like to feed roaches to their animals and feel that they really benefit from eating them. If readers are interested in furthering their education about these insects they should contact a local university that has an entomology department which could assist in locating cockroach cultures. There are some private suppliers of roaches that occasionally advertise them. Expect to pay a considerable sum of money for what you might ordinarily think of as a valueless insect.

Crickets

Crickets belong to a large family of insects that inhabit many habitat niches all over the world. There are mainly three species that have been utilized as feeder insects for many years in Europe and America. They are cultured with relative ease all over the world and are one of the mainstays of the industry. They can be very nutritious when fed correctly and dusted or gut-loaded with minerals and vitamins in order to balance out the high amount of phosphorous that their bodies naturally contain. A lot of chameleon keepers have made the mistake of feeding their crickets on only prepared animal foods such as dog food, monkey chow and poultry meals that contain synthetic vitamins and are high in phosphorous. It is clear at this time that some of these synthetic vitamin products are toxic to lizards of several species and do cause irreversible health problems and even death in some cases. We recommend that all crickets be fed on dark green vegetables such as broccoli and other natural foodstuffs that do not contain these chemicals. Recently the herpetological vitamin and supplement suppliers have recognized the importance of eliminating especially synthetic forms of vitamin A from reptile diets and are adjusting their formulations to include beta carotene which is naturally derived and is a precursor to vitamin A and which is reconverted in the body of reptiles to active vitamin A as needed by the animal. This is a much-welcomed change and has made life simpler for the keeper and healthier for the lizards. There are a couple of problems with the use of beta carotene as a possible source of natural vitamin A in the diets of animals and this includes humans as well. The first problem is that other carotenoids are forgotten for their life-giving properties that we are only now starting to discover. The second problem is that many forms of beta carotene are highly unstable in warm temperatures and will quickly become devalued unless kept frozen. Natural sources of carotene are dark green, yellow, orange and red vegetables which are quite beneficial in adding important ingredients into a feeder insect's diet and then subsequently into the feeding chameleon.

Normally, escaped domestic house crickets are not much of a pest and soon die out when deprived of food and water. They have the advantage of being available in a wide assortment of sizes for all ages and species of chameleons to eat.

Many animals will tire of eating a steady diet of crickets after a while and will stop feeding on them if not offered another dissimilar species of insect. We are currently experimenting with the use of a species of giant black cricket to feed our animals and have found that most animals will run across the room to get to one of these. When our Parson's chameleons tire of eating a diet of the normal brown house crickets, we offer some of these black crickets instead and the response and change in the animals is amazing to behold. Europeans have used these larger species of crickets for years and we have been told many times by European friends that they are more nutritious for animals to eat. Apparently the larger black species contain more fat storage bodies than the desert species such as the common brown cricket. We are sure of one thing—animals that we have tried these crickets on really prefer them over brown house crickets.

Flies

There are thousands of species of flies all over the world and for our purposes we will limit our comments to the main species that are cultivated for fish bait or feeder insects. Currently on the market there are basically three species of flies available. Normally these are sold as maggots and shipped in this stage. The common housefly, the greenbottle fly and the timber fly are all common names given to the species available. These insects vary in size with the housefly being the smallest and the timberfly the largest.

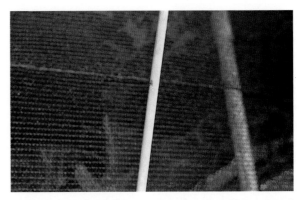

Figure 4.7: Hawaiian fruit fly. The main diet of Hawaiian *C. jacksonii* on the Big Island.

Instructions provided by the suppliers instruct that if the user wants to produce flies for feeding, then the maggots should be kept in the refrigerator and small amounts necessary for feeding be taken out and kept at a warmer temperature where they will quickly develop into flies for feeding. The real trick comes when the keeper tries to get the flies into his chameleon's enclosure without populating his own home with the nuisances. The best way to accomplish this is by taking out an amount of maggots and letting them pupate into an inanimate brown cocoon. Once this has happened they can be placed in a covered small plastic dish (like the ones made for soft margarine) inside the lizard's enclosure. A small hole in the lid can be left open for the emerging flies to escape from. If your chameleon enclosure is screened with fine enough wire they cannot escape and will provide your animals with a challenge to hunt down and devour.

Flies are not known for their superior nutritive values. They are almost valueless to an animal unless gutloaded prior to feeding them to a chameleon. We are currently using a mixture of Miner-All, powdered milk, bee pollen and crushed fruit. Flies found in nature are an entirely different subject when it comes to nutrition for prey animals like lizards. Under natural conditions flies are constantly on the move, searching out food items that are often disgusting to us but nevertheless nutritious and contain many benefits to an animal eating them. An analysis of wild-caught flies versus insectary-raised flies is a real eye opener! The wild flies contain very good nutritional aspects with a calcium to phosphorus ratio approaching what is needed by predatory animals. Flies that are insectary raised and then properly fed on nutritious gutloading food are even superior to the wild fly as a feeder insect, as they will contain proper vitamin and calcium to phosphorus levels. If you do use insectary-raised flies, and you should, always remember to gutload them first before feeding.

Wild flies can be attracted to rotten meat or fish then trapped and fed to animals. Some people use this method and have had no problems with it. We experimented with it and had animals develop mysterious problems akin to what a warm-blooded animal would exhibit from botulism or some other type of food poisoning. Our animals lost the complete use of their tongues and developed severe neurological problems. Since that time we have only used domestically raised flies as a food source.

I write the above caution not to frighten the reader off from using wild-caught insects but as a warning about using insects from unsafe origins. Analysis for toxic insecticides in free-flying flies reveals that these insects can become resistant to many potent poisons and can carry harmful amounts of them around without dying. These toxins are part of the food chain and when these flies are eaten, toxins will build up within the prey animal's body.

Fruit Flies

Fruit flies are absolutely indispensable for the rearing of baby chameleons and smaller species such as the *Brookesia* species of chameleons. There are many forms of fruitflies available for culturing with some mutations and species that have a lot to offer for the chameleon keeper. Wingless, vestigial-winged and large, so-called flightless varieties exist that are not very bothersome if they do escape from the chameleon's enclosure. The regular fruitfly, so common around rotting fruit and other foods that are high in yeasts and sugar content, are easily provided to lizards for food. There are several sources for starter cultures of the various forms. These are offered in various herpetological and tropical fish publications. Usually culturing instructions are provided with the insects by the seller. If you want to use the normal form for feeding

your animals and don't mind escaped insects in your home then they can be cultured by using soft fruits like ripe bananas or potatoes that are placed in an area outside where these insects can find them. After being exposed to the flies for a day or two place the fruit container in your animals' enclosures and sprinkle with a little baker's yeast as food for the larvae. Artificial diets are numerous but usually don't provide as nutritious a base for the flies or the animals eating the flies as the rotting fruit does. Fruitflies are not balanced in regards to calcium to phosphorous ratios and should be gutloaded or sprinkled with a finely powdered mineral source (see Miner-All) prior to feeding. Usually when flies are reared inside of the enclosure along with the chameleons, dusting is not practical or possible, so gutloading is really the only way one has to assure proper mineralization.

Grasshoppers and Locusts

Grasshoppers and locusts are rarely available to the trade in this country. They are extremely good food for a wide amount of herpetological species. In Europe there are two species of locusts raised for this purpose and many longtime breeders feed little else to their animals. In the United States, these insects are used for biomedical and pesticide research and are costly to produce and noncompetitive compared to mealworms and crickets as a feeder insect for the market. We know of only a couple of sources for these insects and one of these companies will hopefully be able to offer them to the animal trade for feeding in the near future. As an additional treat for chameleons, grasshoppers and locusts are truly appreciated by the animals who recognize them as a naturally found insect in their home ranges. It doesn't take many of these insects to fill up a chameleon so they really are not so costly after all, as it would take quite a few more crickets to equal the same amount of food depending on the size of the crickets and the animals being fed. Wild-caught grasshoppers are an excellent food and we have never seen any problems associated with their use. We do caution though that there are species of grasshoppers that are toxic and noxious but in every case that we have tried these experimentally, the animals instinctively knew already not to eat them or would spit them out as soon as they tasted them. If you do feed grasshoppers or locusts to your animals, you should also consider the risk of insecticides that have accumulated in the bodies of these wild-caught grasshoppers. Tests on insects in rural areas, surrounding farms, etc., often show high amounts of insecticides in their bodies to which they have built immunities and are not affected by. On the other hand, the lizards eating these insects have no tolerance for these poisons and will be effected by them. In the case of wild-caught grasshoppers and locusts versus cage-reared ones as a food source I would recommend the latter if possible, unless you are completely sure of their total freedom from insecticides.

Maggots

Maggots are the larvae of flies of all kinds. For our purposes we are referring to the species normally known as houseflies, greenbottle and timberflies. These larvae are specially developed to eat and live in rotten flesh, fruit and other detritus and as such are both beneficial and repugnant. As a source of food they are practically useless for reptiles because they are for the most part indigestible. The reason for this indigestibility involves the tough outer skin covering the maggot's body. This skin is naturally impervious to strong enzymes and other digestive juices otherwise the maggot could not live in dead carcasses or living wounds where strong enzymes are present. Bird-keepers in Europe discovered that by pricking the skin of maggots and then feeding them to their birds they could get complete digestion by their birds. If the chameleon keeper wants to perform this task on the much cleaner cultivated maggot he would find them to be a good source of nutrients to his lizards. Maggots have large fat storage bodies and are an excellent source of energy to an animal that can digest them. Our experience with maggots has been to let them turn into flies and then feed them to our lizards once gutloaded. We feel it is too much trouble and a waste of time to pierce the skin of every maggot fed to a lizard. Once pierced, the maggot soon dies or ceases to wiggle so its attraction to a chameleon is zilch anyway.

Praying Mantis

Mantises are not often thought of as food for lizards but are highly prized by chameleons that seem to recognize them immediately as food. Not generally available to the trade for food, they are best collected when seen and then immediately fed to a waiting mouth.

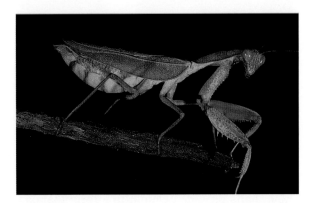

Figure 4.8: Praying mantis. *Photo: David Adamson*

Silkworms

These fat and juicy worms that feed on the leaves of the mulberry tree are one of the closest to perfect feeder insects one could provide to their animals. Silkworms are especially nutritious when gutloaded with mulberry leaf material. These worms are rarely available in the trade on a commercial basis for feeding but eggs can be purchased from scientific supply houses and then hatched and grown on fresh mulberry leaves. Hopefully these worms will become available in the future for those collectors who care about providing their animals with the best food possible.

Snails

Snails occur in two forms, the land snail group and the water snail group. We will be addressing the land snails here. As a food source for mainly montane species of chameleons these mollusks are fantastic. They are the main food source for introduced Jackson's chameleons in southern California locations and they are also eaten in Kenya where the Jackson's normally come from. Other montane species of chameleons such as Johnston's, Werner's and Meller's chameleons seem to relish them also. In southern California and other parts of the

Figure 4.9: Male *C. oshaughnessyi* eating.

United States where they have been introduced, the European brown snail is a common garden inhabitant and is the species that we use. This is the popular species used all over the world as the human delicacy, escargot. Brown snails are nutritious and eat plant materials of all kinds. Their shells provide calcium in a form that can be digested for those species that consume it.

Although all species of snails are carriers of certain parasites, these do not appear to be a major problem with the chameleons. Parasites such as flukes that use water snails as their hosts do not seem to be a problem with the common European brown snails or for that matter with any other species of land snail. We know of no parasite problems as a result of feeding land snails to chameleons and recommend them highly for those species that will consume them.

Tomato and Tobacco Hornworms

Hornworms are incredible feeder insects for the species that like them, which are most of the chameleon species. Their fat and soft-skinned bodies are nutritious and will sustain a thin or sick animal like nothing else. Hornworms are a naturally occurring pest species found throughout the United States and there are other species found in Europe and Asia. These worms usually eat toxic plant parts such as tomato and tobacco leaves and as a result take up these plant toxins into their own systems and become toxic to predators as well. Because of this it is only recommended that hornworms that are reared on artificial diets be used for feeding to your animals. When a source of these insects can be located it is one of the most treasured connections a chameleon keeper could possibly have.

Generally not available to the trade at this time, we hope this will soon change. Hornworms are expensive to rear artificially and take a while to mature so they are priced accordingly. They are well worth searching out and buying just to see the smile they put on an animal's face (figuratively speaking of course).

We gutload these worms on ripe tomato fruit before giving them to our animals and they quickly plump up from this as they are usually a little dehydrated when we first receive them. They are deficient in calcium and trace elements and need to be dusted with an appropriate preparation to increase their nutritive value.

Waxworms

Waxworms are actually the larvae of a moth species that inhabits honeycombs of infested honeybee colonies. These pests are much hated by bee keepers as they are very destructive to the wax combs within the hive. As a food they are excellent for fattening thin animals and as an occasional treat for others. Waxworms have soft skins which are easily broken and digested by all lizards. Nutritionally, they lack minerals and will need to be dusted for the best nutritive results. Some species of chameleons like them more than others. They are usually delivered from the supplier in sawdust which they don't eat and they are starving when received. Waxworms are not as nutritious as some other species of insects and small chameleons have been known to choke on them so caution is advised.

Zophobias or Giant Mealworms

This naturally occurring mealwormlike species was introduced to herpetoculture a few years ago by European insect breeders. It originated in Central America and belongs to a large family of tenebroid beetles that also includes the common mealworm. For many years a large version of the common mealworm has been available in the United States, but this insect was nothing more than a hormone-induced giant. Even today these mutants exist and should not be confused with the Zophobia giant mealworm.

The Zophobia worm is an excellent feeder insect for chameleons that are large enough to handle it. These worms are strong and have a chewing ability that could possibly be hazardous to an animal that does not kill the worm before swallowing it. Stories are told of these insects eating their way through the body wall from the inside of an animal. We have been using them for years and have never had any problem with them at all. I have watched over and over again to see if our chameleons swallow these worms whole and every time they chew them well before swallowing which effectively kills the worms. Zophobias are readily accepted by most chameleons and are easily maintained for long periods of time on bran as a base and then fed all types of other food items which they consume readily. They are deficient in minerals like most insects and need gutloading or dusting. We know of animals that have existed almost entirely on these worms for a long time. Although I don't recommend this as a general practice it does show how effective nutrient loading can be with a single food source.

I intentionally left the common mealworm off this list of insects, not because it shouldn't be considered by keepers but its qualities are already well known and in our experience we have had better response and acceptance from our animals with the giant mealworm over its diminutive cousin. Zophobias do not require refrigeration, as it will kill them very quickly if

Figure 4.10: Male *C. parsonii* eating.

used. They are far more active and proportionally are reputed to contain less chitin (hard outer skin) and be more digestible. We have not verified these claims but these worms do seem softer and appear to contain more digestible body parts other than just a tough skin. (See back matter for a list of food suppliers.)

Vitamin and Mineral Supplementation

Today knowledge about breeding and keeping reptiles is so far advanced from what it was only a few years ago that it seems as though a totally new era has arrived in the keeping and breeding of reptiles in captivity. With all of this increased information it is equally astounding how little has been learned about the nutritional aspects required by many of the reptiles in our care.

When we began raising chameleons we started by buying a live-bearing species (Jackson's chameleon, *C. jacksonii*) which gave us many offspring over time. Newborn chameleons are among the most endearing of creatures and it was very heart breaking to see many of these die from what seemed to be some sort of viral or neurological disorder. After a lot of research and networking with other breeders we found out that the disorders we were seeing were caused from imbalances in the mineral and vitamin components of our chameleons' diets. After discovering this, we began a search for the proper commercial products that would remedy the situation. It seemed logical that these deficiency problems could be obliterated based on the knowledge that the problem was solely nutritional.

Our first mistake was the total acceptance of what the self-proclaimed experts had told us to use in order to remedy the problems we were having. In some cases we were advised to accept some deformities or deaths as this was normal with chameleons. It truly was a case of the blind leading the blind. We tried one brand after another of so-called "complete" calcium and vitamin products formulated exclusively for the reptile and amphibian market. Eventually we did get better results and were finally able to raise some newborns to adulthood but something was still wrong. The animals that we were raising were not at all like their wild-caught counterparts. Our captive-reared youngsters had skin textures that were noticeably smoother and lacked the characteristic bumpiness and rough texture of their wild cousins. The captive-reared lizards also lacked that indescribable spark of vigor that a wild caught animal has. At this juncture, we were also being told by the "experts" that these conditions were normal and this was the way that domestics were supposed to be. "After all, their skins were in better condition because they didn't have to endure the harsh environments that the wild animals do." We were told that their lackluster behavior corresponded to being raised in captivity where they were used to people. We did not buy these explanations for one minute! After networking with other breeders we discovered that many of them were experiencing exactly the same problems we were. They were also seeing breeding depression after a couple of generations, during which their animals would apparently go sterile and no longer reproduce.

We had followed nutritional research in humans for years and had a rudimentary knowledge of how nutrients could possibly be at the root of these problems. After discussing these symptoms with a friend of ours who had experience in formulation of natural animal supplements and who also kept and bred reptiles, it was decided that he would work on the problem and see what could be done. After a few months he appeared at our door with a large bag of white, fine powder and asked us to use it for the next year. Our instructions were to dust every feeder insect in an effort to load them with nutrients prior to feeding. We were to use it only on animals kept indoors and on all ages of chameleons. He also asked us to keep notes and to run the experiment with test controls. We noticed an immediate difference between this product and any others we had been using, it stuck to the exoskeleton of the insects much better and longer and was accepted without any resistance from the lizards. After only a few months of eating insects dusted with this powder our hatchlings were so different from what we had been producing that we knew we were on the right track. We no longer had metabolic bone

Figure 4.11: Juvenile *C. jacksonii* male.

disease even in animals that could not be taken outside for exposure to the sunlight. Growth problems such as dwarfing and deformities became a thing of the past, in fact these animals grew almost twice as fast as our control animals. Even larger animals that were experiencing the beginnings of metabolic bone disease recovered completely from their deficient conditions.

When we asked what was in this incredible powder our friend would only say that the product was totally natural and consisted of ingredients that these animals would normally consume in the wild. That wasn't good enough, we nagged and cajoled, at one point we jokingly offered our firstborn in trade for the secret. Finally we came to a business agreement that would allow us to distribute the product to others so that they could also benefit from its use. After we were given the actual ingredient list along with the reasoning for formulating such a supplement it became clear why this product worked so well for us. The microfine powder consisted of not only just calcium carbonate but also other minerals and many trace elements that we now understand are so vital to an animal's well being. A mineral and trace mineral analysis of deceased wild-caught chameleon's skin, muscle and bone has substantiated that the need for all of these nutrients is not only real but absolutely necessary! When these analytical tests were made and minerals and microminerals were found within the cellular walls of tissue from wild chameleons, it made sense that these probably had some purpose for being there. Through this important research it has became clear that the best approach to proper reptile nutrition in captivity is to follow what the animals are getting in nature.

Commercial insect-rearing businesses keep their insects on diets that usually do not contain all of the important trace elements needed for chameleons and other reptiles over their life spans. These insects are raised over countless generations on food that the particular insects require to breed and grow on and with only the bare essentials to accomplish this. With the introduction of Miner-All (our product name) the need for multimineral and trace elements could be filled by dusting these deficient insects prior to feeding chameleons.

Miner-All was purposefully formulated not to contain a blend of vitamins with the minerals. It does contain vitamin D3 for proper calcium absorption, however. Studies in nutrition have shown that when vitamins and minerals are mixed together without fillers separating them they quickly begin reacting with each other much like they do when eaten. Vitamins begin this process called chelation soon after being combined with mineral components whether in the stomach or outside it. The combination of these nutrients outside of the body begins a process that devalues both nutrient factors considerably before they can be assimilated within the body. It is important to understand that vitamins and minerals do work together in the body for the benefit of the consuming animal but they should be taken separately to avoid contact subsequent to use.

One of the problems we discovered very early in the chameleon-raising game was that all of the mineral supplements on the market meant for reptiles and amphibians, included vitamin D3 for proper calcium utilization by the animals consuming them. Even though this vitamin is very important, it can often be over utilized and can cause animals to absorb far too much calcium over a short period of time. Normally lizards manufacture their own vitamin D3 when exposed to natural sunlight without it passing

Figure 4.12: Tomato horn worm, Zophobia worm and cricket coated with Miner-All.

through glass or plastic. When this process happens in nature the animals only manufacture the amount that is needed to fulfill their needs for calcium absorption. When our animals were supplemented with the existing products and then taken outside for the summer we found that they were receiving vitamin D3 from the supplements as well as manufacturing more on their own as a result of exposure to the sun. Many of these animals were experiencing severe health problems as a result and sometimes would die after only a couple of months of overdosing on vitamin D3. Chameleons that died were autopsied and found to have all of the classic symptoms of vitamin D poisoning. In some cases organs such as the kidneys were calcified and almost bonelike, intestines were also becoming hardened and nonfunctional.

We now advise every keeper of any reptile or amphibian to be careful and only use supplementation with vitamin D3 when these animals are housed exclusively indoors without the

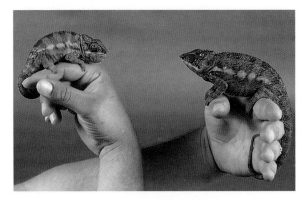

Figure 4.13: Size and squamation difference of same age captive-bred and wild-caught, blue morph *C. pardalis*.

benefit of receiving unfiltered sunlight. Soon after we began using the Miner-All product for our inside animals, which contained vitamin D3, we realized that this supplement would not suit the purposes of our animals housed out of doors for periods of eight hours or more per week. It was not long before we had exactly the same formulation of Miner-All without vitamin D3 manufactured and it has really been a very helpful ingredient in managing our outside animals.

Author's note: If the above information looks like a self-serving commercial for our own product I can only say that it is not meant for this purpose. I agonized over writing it at all, but I also felt responsible to give the very best information to readers in an effort to help chameleons and their health.

I assure you that if I did not have any personal interest in this product and it was available from another manufacturer I would be singing its praises just as much as I have our product. I cannot consciously recommend any other existing product for the purpose of supplying minerals to reptiles because I now understand the importance of total nutrition for these animals and other products have only addressed a small part of this picture. Some of the products on the market have shown on analysis to contain very high levels of heavy metals which are toxic. These are usually a result of using oyster shell for the calcium source. Oysters are filter feeders and absorb large amounts of ocean-based pollutants as a result. Other products contain calcium from sources such as bone meal, that are not digestible by most reptiles and amphibians. These particular products were originally intended for use by animals that can digest bone but certainly have little place in the nutritional needs of reptiles and amphibians.

No doubt other products will surface in the future that will be attuned to the specific needs of

reptiles and we will be experimenting with these also. Hopefully in future reprints I can promote these products as much as I have our own.

When asked about the use of Miner-All we suggest that all insects intended for feeding to animals should be placed in a small, covered container and a small amount of Miner-All sprinkled on them for coating the outside of every insect. These insects should be fed immediately and only in the amounts needed for each animal.

The incorrect supplementation of a chameleon's diet with many synthetic vitamins has resulted in the loss of life to untold numbers of chameleons in captivity. These nutrients when used improperly are toxic and create health problems on their own. Long-term overdosing causes ulceration of the liver, stomach and intestinal lining, along with life-threatening edemas of the organs and especially the thyroid gland. The subject of vitamin supplementation of chameleons deserves a lot more research than what it has received to date. These lizards are far more sensitive to these nutrients than perhaps any other known species of reptiles.

It is vital that new products coming onto the market address the problems created by the overuse of vitamins on reptiles and try to cover all of the bases before we find that we have lost all of our breeding stock and can't get any more because they cannot be imported any longer. We find gutloading insects on fresh fruits and vegetables the best way to get vitamins into the animals.

Anybody looking for a vitamin product that will be good for their animals should only contemplate using a vitamin product that has been manufactured using vitamins derived from natural sources. Vitamin A should be avoided like the plague. Beta carotene has replaced this lizard killer in several products and more improvements in formulations are around the bend.

5

Chameleon Health

A friend of mine once made the observation that if you keep live animals you will have sick and dead animals. Truer words were never spoken! It really does not matter what animal species you keep, whether it be a dog or a chameleon the above adage will apply. Although chameleons have received a bad rap when it comes to their long-term health and happiness in captivity, they really aren't much different from any other wild-caught animal taken from its habitat, often starved and deprived of water then shipped in a tight, dark unfamiliar container for sometimes days. When they finally do arrive they are often taken directly from the box they were imported in and repacked without water, food or rest into another crate and shipped again to another destination. Upon arriving at this destination which is usually a pet store, the animals are often placed either in crowded conditions with other chameleons or reptile species or handled like a new toy by employees and clients with little regard for what they have just gone through. Delicate? Nonsense! Try putting a few strong human beings through this treatment and see how many of them survive! It isn't very difficult to understand why so many of these animals die needlessly when the story could be much different for them. A little compassion and consideration along the way would work wonders for the overall fitness of these imported creatures.

We know friends who have lived in Africa and who have kept chameleons there. They are amazed that these lizards have such a reputation for being delicate here. In Africa these animals are as hardy as any other lizard and often kept in the garden as a form of pest control.

It is interesting that often strong and apparently healthy chameleons are packed and shipped all over the world but shortly after they are unpacked they begin to experience health problems. Usually these problems are a direct result of stress, both psychological and physical, and an already pre-existing parasite load that is now literally exploding in numbers within their bodies. Soon other secondary infections follow, if these hapless animals live that long, and eventually many perish. It is the treatment and care of these compromised animals and their health problems that is the main focus of this chapter. There are many health conditions that are too complex for treatment by the average chameleon keeper and these should be seen by a veterinarian experienced in reptile health care. I will attempt to cover some of the more common health problems in this chapter but do encourage the reader to seek professional help for difficult problems. Often a chameleon keeper will call us and ask for a certain treatment involving antibiotic therapy. Usually the person on the other end of the line hasn't a clue what a milligram or a milliliter is, let alone have the knowledge of how to use these medications correctly. Unless the reader is absolutely certain of what they are doing and are versed in medical matters involving injections, oral dosing, etc. They should not waste their time or their valuable animal's life practicing on it. If the need for antibiotics does arise and the correct antibiotic can be determined to treat the malady, it is important that the chameleon owner knows how to treat and for how long. If the keeper has a good rapport with his veterinarian he can often get rudimentary training there. If the veterinarian is averse to training a novice, and believe me some are, then the next best bet is finding another veterinarian or learning from a competent breeder that has experience in these matters.

Using antibiotics is like using a two-edged sword. They can be of immense help to an animal that needs them but they can also kill or damage an animal when used by a person who does not understand their proper usage. A good example of a drug that can be a real life saver or a slow killer is Ivermectin. We have seen animals only slightly overdosed, die from the misuse of this drug by their owners. There are other wonder drugs that have saved many animals but also have been misused and as a result have killed animals. Be very sure that you understand the repercussions of a particular drug before using it. There are several books extensively written on reptile diseases and some of the better titles can be located in the bibliography of this book.

Anyone keeping any species of wild animal should familiarize themselves with the rudimentary needs of a sick creature. In the case of chameleons this is absolutely essential if the ill animal has any chance of surviving. Often it is the first aid of the keeper that has led to the eventual rehabilitation of a once sick animal. I recommend the following suggestions be followed in the event of an emergency.

Keep the name and number of an experienced veterinarian that will treat your animal with the proper procedure if needed near your lizard's enclosure. Have a separate hospital cage for housing the sick animal(s). Have an area away from other animals that could become exposed. This area should be stress free and in a quiet and temperature-controlled location.

The following items should be acquired by the experienced keeper versed in medical treatment and therapeutic practices:

1. Two or more small milliliter syringes of 1 cc volume with needles and a few without.

2. Two larger syringes each with 3 cc volumes or more, two with needles and two without.

3. A container of injectable Lactated-Ringers solution and oral Pedialite are an absolute must in the medicine chest.

4. Polysporin and Neosporin ointment.

5. Injectable 5 percent baytril (for the more experienced keeper).

6. Emeraid by LaFaber (very important), other caloric/carbohydrate preparations can also be stocked.

7. For the more experienced, the following two drugs: Flagyl (150 ml) and 10 percent Panacur worming paste.

First aid action is absolutely essential when it is noticed that a chameleon is not acting normally. If the animal seems overly listless or extremely restless something is certainly causing this condition. Determining what is listless or overactive is difficult for the beginner for sure, but if he is lucky enough to have experienced a healthy animal in the beginning he will be able to determine what is normal behavior and what is not. Sometimes the animal will be exhibiting darker color than usual or will in some other way act ill at ease. The most dangerous situation in caring for a sick animal is that the keeper will spend precious time denying that anything is wrong and the animal's condition will steadily deteriorate until nothing can be done for it. It is sometimes very difficult for even the experienced breeder to determine what is the cause and cure for a mystery condition in one of his animals. In some of these cases the condition will right itself and in others it will not. The trick to helping any animal is being able to learn its habits so well that any unusual behavior becomes suspect. A good veterinarian will have developed a second sense for determining what is correct behavior and what is not, before he considers medical treatment of an unfamiliar animal. Imagine being in his position and never having had any prior experience with this particular species. The private keeper, if at all talented, can acquire this same second sense for his animal charges and this sense will serve him well.

When administering a treatment of antibiotics

to a chameleon it is important to realize that even after a couple of days of treatment the animal may show no sign of recovery. Chameleons are extremely slow to recover from most illnesses and sometimes it is weeks after a course of antibiotic treatment before one really knows if it worked or not.

It is always important to keep a sick animal away from others, in totally separate quarters. During treatment the sick animal should be maintained at the higher end of its normal temperature range. This will facilitate its body functions to better utilize the antibiotics given to it. Some drugs will not work effectively in lower temperatures and need to be checked for this characteristic. The following is a brief list of the more common conditions, diseases and infections that we have encountered.

External conditions and parasites:

> Mites and ticks (very rare on chameleons)
> Eye infections
> Sunken eyes

Internal conditions and parasites:

> Nematodes (roundworms), cestodes (tapeworms), filarians (threadworms), flukes
> Gastroenteritis
> Metabolic bone disease

Mouth infection:

> Mouthrot
> Mouth lesions
> Infected or injured tongue

Trauma to or swelling of appendages

Respiratory infection

Home Remedies

Although my experience and advice for treating and curing some infections and diseases may not be approved by all veterinarians they have worked well for us and I will pass them on to you. It should be noted that even among veterinarians there is often disagreement about treatment disciplines. I have been extremely fortunate to work very closely with a couple of veterinarians who have been equally willing to work with me in order to develop safe dosages and administration of drugs to cure chameleon-specific diseases and infections. Dr. Scott J. Stahl, D.V.M. of Fairfax, Virginia, has been an invaluable source of information on dosages and possible surgical cures for ailments that we have encountered. Dr. Warren Whalen of Temecula, California, has also provided us with options we would not have been able to explore without his help on more occasions then I care to count.

The following remedies have worked for other breeders, as well as ourselves. All chameleon medical treatments are experimental at this time, and until we have had several years of scientific evaluation, it will out of necessity be common sense and experimentation that will determine how we will treat these animals.

Eye Infections

A chameleon uses its eyes much as we do and when they experience an infection or other mishap associated with their eyes they are severely affected by not being able to see. Eye infections quite often will lead to a climate for unhealthy psychological problems, if not treated immedi-

Figure 5.1: Male *C. jacksonii* with his tail bit off by rats in the jungle of Hawaii.

Figure 5.2: Female *C. pardalis* with a severe eye infection.

ately. Normally an eye infection will begin by fusing one of the chameleon's eyes shut, often with visible matter. Hopefully the chameleon will continue drinking and attempting to eat in this condition and the treatment, if begun quickly, will arrest the problem and it will not spread to the other eye. In either situation, if the problem affects one or both eyes the treatment will be the same. We begin treatment by first giving the animal a shower in slow-flowing, tepid water for a period of one hour. Usually this will loosen the matter and often the eye will become totally unplugged from just this treatment alone, as this is the natural way that chameleons clean their eyes. If this does not work, then we apply the appropriate eye ointment as follows. If the softened matter is still present we then moisten a cotton swab with sterile saline solution, and roll it across the infected eye using gentle pressure. Do this until the eye is finally open, a plug of matter may be seen covering the eye itself. Very gently remove the matter with the end of the cotton swab. After all of the matter has been cleaned out, apply a small amount of teramycin eye ointment directly onto the eye. This can be purchased in pet stores or feed stores catering to horse or cattle clients. If you cannot find it elsewhere it certainly can be obtained from a veterinarian.

In the event that there is no matter covering the eye, apply the ointment directly onto the eye, and repeat once a day until the condition clears. Continue the treatment for a further five days past the time that the infection has disappeared. Normally this should take approximately one week. If after this treatment time the eye is still fusing shut, consult a chameleon-experienced veterinarian immediately. A second drug that we have had excellent luck with is Gentocin eye ointment (nonsteroidal). This should be used under the watchful eye of your veterinarian who can determine whether or not this drug is indicated for the particular eye condition your animal has.

Mouthrot

This condition is exactly that, a condition and not a specific disease in and of itself. Mouthrot can be the result of a trauma wound to the gums or lips that has become infected or an infection

Figure 5.3: Male *C. globifer* with mouthrot.

appearing in the mouth as a result of a systemic bacteria. Several bacterial organisms can cause symptoms of mouthrot and it is very important to realize that what might treat and cure one animal of this malady might not work on another with the same symptoms. In most cases of mouthrot, or infectious stomatitis as it is medically referred to, the condition manifests itself by causing swelling and areas of discoloration within the mucus membranes of the mouth. Often the first sign of it comes with the animal holding its mouth slightly open or showing a sensitivity to anything touching the sore areas. Many times the animal will stop feeding because of the pain caused from mastication of food. It is extremely important to treat these areas when you first notice them. If the infection is caused from a very potent strain of bacteria it can quickly travel into the jaw bone and erode it. Once this occurs, the chances of saving the animal are minimal, although not impossible.

Figure 5.4: Forcing a *C. globifer* male to gape.

Look for white or yellow caseous matter on the areas around the inner jaw line, and in the soft inner lining of the corners of the mouth. If the abscess is protruding out from the normal surface level of the surrounding tissue try to gently remove it with a cotton-tipped swab. If it resists removal then puncture the top of the abscess with a sterile syringe needle first and then remove the caseous matter with the cotton swab. The wound might bleed slightly but this is usually of little concern. Prepare a syringe with povidone iodine or chlorhexidine diacetate (brand name Nolvasan) available from veterinary supply houses. Using a syringe, gently irrigate the wound with this solution after removing any caseous material from the site. This treatment might be sufficient and after a few treatments the condition will clear up. In cases where the disease is more advanced or the causative organism is not sensitive to the above treatment the more powerful drug therapy might be needed. Injectable Baytril 5 percent solution (the dosage rates are at the end of the chapter) has been useful in some cases when it is used to irrigate the area of the infection. This will be required for a period of 10 days in order to affect a cure.

We have also used a salve called Silvadine cream with great success in the treatment of most cases of mouthrot. This is used topically on the cleaned wound area for a period of 10 consecutive days. It has been suggested in literature that the addition of injectable vitamin C at a rate of 10–20 mg per kilo has been also effective in aiding the eradication of this disease condition.

We have had several heated conversations with knowledgeable chameleon keepers regarding the reasons for an animal developing mouthrot conditions. Our view is that this condition normally appears in an animal that has a severely depressed immune condition. This usually is a result of acute stress caused from a whole host of conditions. We have seen animals with severe mouthrot conditions spontaneously healed when placed in a habitat that suited them better than the one they were in previously. An animal who has an immune system that is compromised will often have a metabolism that is not up to par either, but outdoor sunlight helps to build up this immune system. One of our suspicions is that stressed animals that do not have access to natural sunlight are much more prone to mouthrot conditions. Chameleons who are ill will slow their body processes and quite often will not eat or defecate in a normal manner.

Upper-respiratory Infection

Probably the most serious illnesses that we have had to deal with in our animals are upper-respiratory infections. These are certain killers if not diagnosed and treated in time. Symptoms include bubbles in the mouth, or stringy mucus just under the lips at the gum line. Sometimes the keeper can hear a wheezing or popping sound coming from the lungs. Advanced stages are often demonstrated by the appearance of the animal drooling a thick, clear liquid while drinking or open-mouth breathing. Drooling can be misleading especially if the chameleon is not hydrated every day. An animal that is dehydrated will often exhibit drooling of mucus-filled saliva when drinking. Since drooling is a sign of both an upper-respiratory infection and severe dehydration, it is important to be aware of the chameleon's water intake in order to make an accurate diagnosis.

Early detection is often difficult for the new chameleon owner, but is crucial for the survival of the chameleon. Signs to look for are the following: open-mouth breathing, sneezing, coughing, wheezing and/or forced exhalation with a rattlelike sound. Often the animal has sunken eyes, refuses to drink or eat and green or yellow crusty matter appears from the nostrils. When forced to gape, look for stringy mucus or bubbles in the throat. If your chameleon has been drinking well, assume that it has an upper-respiratory infection especially when accompanied by other signs from the above list.

It is important to inspect the newly acquired chameleon at least once a week for the above signs. This inspection schedule should take place from the time the chameleon is first brought into the home, and for a period of several weeks thereafter. These infections sometimes don't exhibit outward signs for sometime and it is always good to keep a watchful eye on the animal until after it becomes well established. After the owner gets to know the animal he will be able to quickly determine any unusual signs of distress or illness.

Upper-respiratory infections as well as most other acute illnesses normally need to be treated with a course of antibiotic therapy. During the use of these medications it is important to remember that chameleons will often go off their food and it is especially important to make sure that they stay well hydrated during treatment. They can go without food for several days to a couple of weeks but they certainly cannot do without water. If a sick animal does become dehydrated, it is imperative to get vital fluids into its body. Some time ago we became familiar with a product manufactured for rehydration of compromised animals that can be administered orally and has worked like a charm for us. The product is Emeraid 1 (a carbohydrate booster formulated for birds) it is not generally available to anyone other then veterinarians but usually can be obtained from them. If it is not possible to obtain Emeraid, then a less satisfactory but still useful substitute would be pedialyte (obtained from the infant section in the supermarket). When administering oral fluids to a dehydrated animal it is important to know how much fluid to give during treatment. I usually try to estimate this amount by visualizing the size of the ill chameleon's stomach. Normally this organ is quite small, and so I offer small amounts of fluids more frequently and do not try to give a single large dose at one time. I find that absorption is better when following this method. Try offering a dehydrated chameleon a couple of cc at a time, over a few hours.

For severe dehydration, where the animal has sunken eyes and is not responding well to oral dosing, it is absolutely imperative that fluids be given subcutaneously immediately. We usually find that a chameleon that cannot swallow fluids willingly must be dosed in this manner. If the keeper is not comfortable with injection procedures on his animals then he should contract an experienced collector or veterinarian to do this task. The important thing to remember is that the procedure must be done very soon in order to save the animal's life! Once an animal is determined to be severely dehydrated there is

little time left before the kidneys will be affected and the point of no return is reached.

Injection of Lactated-Ringers with 5 percent dextrose under the skin will often bring a critically dehydrated animal back from the edge fairly quickly. We have seen animals that were nearly dead revived with this treatment, but it must be done with a good knowledge of injection therapy. In the hands of an inexperienced person the treatment could prove to be deadly. Lactated-Ringers solution given subcutaneously quickly hydrates the chameleon by being absorbed without having to first pass through the gut lining. A sick animal often is unable to absorb anything through its inflamed intestinal lining and injection by the above method will bypass the oral route and gets the fluid into the lizard's system more efficiently. Lactated-Ringers solution is available with prescription from some pharmacies or through a veterinarian that recognizes the importance of the serious chameleon keeper having this life-saving fluid available in the home for first aid measures.

The above-mentioned "body shut down" is primarily the reason we do not recommend that oral antibiotics be given with the more advanced infections. However, oral administration is far less stressful to the chameleon, and it works well with mild cases of disease which is usually the case in treating mouthrot.

Metabolic Bone Disease

This commonly encountered disease is the result of a growing chameleon's inability to metabolize available calcium and other minerals or the lack of these minerals in sufficient quantities to enable the animal to absorb them properly. At one time this disease spelled doom to almost all lizards and lizard collections where these animals were being kept indoors. Metabolic bone disease (MBD) used to be considered incurable and caused huge losses in animals being raised indoors without the benefit of the sun and adequate amounts of absorbable calcium. Even today, years after the discovery of the cause of this hideous disease, an untreated chameleon contracting this malady will be doomed to a short life of crippled existence. Unless the symptoms are recognized in the very beginning stages of the disease and aggressive, remedial

Figure 5.5: Metabolic bone disease in a female *C. calyptratus.*

treatment is started immediately, there can be little hope of rescuing an animal from deformation of its skeleton and possibly other permanent manifestations of the disease. Even with immediate treatment of an animal in the beginning stages we have seen permanent disfigurement of the facial structure as well as unsightly skin blemishes and defects.

Even though early detection of symptoms is vital to effecting an early reversal of the disorder, prevention is the real key to successfully keeping these animals healthy. If the chameleon keeper will become familiar with the importance of giving quality mineral supplementation that includes calcium as well as other minerals and micronutrients, this disease will never rear its hideous head.

A brief course into the mechanics of how this disease originates might be helpful to the reader. As mentioned at the beginning of this section, the disease is a result of a reptile not being able to absorb enough calcium and other minerals for proper functioning of its musculoskeletal system. This absorption problem is normally the result of an animal not receiving enough ultraviolet rays of the proper intensity from the sun. Without these beneficial rays the lizard cannot synthesize vitamin D3 within its body. Vitamin D3 enables the lizard's body to absorb calcium properly and to deposit it in its bones, muscles and skin as needed. Often captive reptiles are not provided the opportunity to expose themselves to natural, unfiltered sunlight of the correct intensity and for periods of time that are sufficient for the creation of vita-

min D3. Reptiles as well as most known mammals and birds that do not have access to unfiltered sunlight must be given vitamin D3 in their diets. Without this artificial supplementation they will eventually develop metabolic bone disease. We generally recommend that a chameleon be exposed to unfiltered sunlight for at least eight hours weekly or be supplemented with a mineral supplement that contains vitamin D3 in it. On the other hand, a chameleon that is exposed to unfiltered sunlight must also receive calcium as well as other minerals but the use of vitamin D3 should be avoided or mineralization of organs and other soft tissues will occur. Vitamin D3 in its synthetic form is quite toxic when overdosed. It is extremely important to follow the instructions on the label of any product containing this vitamin. It should also be remembered that insects fed on diets rich in vitamin D3 should not be given to chameleons that are kept outside and exposed to the sun as these will act as further supplementation and could prove to be either toxic or cause overmineralization of the tissues or organs.

Metabolic bone disease can most often be seen in chameleons that are rapidly growing. As the animals grow, their bones must take in minerals for strength and support of the rest of the body parts. When a young chameleon is fed an abundance of food that has not been properly treated by gutloading, dusting or both, the chameleon will metabolize this food and will grow without receiving the much-needed minerals for its bones. Young chameleons that are fed in moderation will grow more slowly and are far less likely to contract metabolic bone disease as a result. As a chameleon reaches its full size as an adult the need for minerals decreases. Calcium and mineral needs increase with adult animals under stress or in the case of females developing eggs when the need again for calcium and other minerals is high.

From the time that a chameleon hatches until it reaches the subadult stage of its life, it should receive calcium and other minerals with every feeding. In the subadult stage (three-quarters grown), the mineral needs lessen and I recommend that these animals receive mineral supplementation at every other feeding. For an adult that is not stressed or producing eggs I recommend that minerals be given at every third feeding. In the case of a female that has just laid eggs, minerals should be given on every feeding until the female is restored to her previous vitality, normally about 10 days after egg laying.

I am often asked the question of what is meant by unfiltered sunlight? Anytime that sunlight passes through a blockade whether it be a screen or glass it looses some of its beneficial ultraviolet rays. Glass especially, will completely block the rays from passing through it and animals placed nearby a glass window with the intention that this will provide sufficient ultraviolet radiation will not benefit from the sun other then to receive solar heating.

Animals placed outside, where they can be exposed to direct sunlight, will receive the most benefit from it. It is important to note that even animals that are outside and are under shade such as a tree, will get sufficient ultraviolet to manufacture vitamin D3, but to what extent I am not certain. Probably the best thing a chameleon keeper can do for his animals in this case, is to provide a place for full-sun basking as well as a place for the animal to shade itself in order to keep from overheating.

We have seen examples of what could be described as metabolic bone disease but were not caused from inadequate dietary calcium/vitamin D3 or sunlight exposure. Some of these cases defy explanation. Sometimes when we question the owner of a suffering animal everything seems to be correct on the surface but upon closer examination the problem is often that the owner has neglected giving newborn, infant, gravid and subadult chameleons proper amounts of calcium and minerals in their diet. Usually we find these collectors have been using products meant for dogs and cats made from bone ash and that these were not being absorbed properly and resulted in deformed animals. Another possible cause of deformation appears to be the inbreeding of siblings over several generations or possibly improper nutrition over generations. This seems to be one problem with the captive population of veiled chameleons, *Chamaeleo calyptratus*. We see this species with more genetic metabolic bone disease than

any other chameleon species. Often female veiled chameleons are fed far too often and with huge amounts of insects which results in their bodies growing far too rapidly for their bone growth to keep up with.

We have seen immature female chameleons whose bodies were full of fertile eggs and whose bones were so demineralized that their legs could be physically bent at a forty-five degree angle like a piece of rubber. We have always found these animals difficult to rehabilitate and generally recommend euthanizing them. If the female seems to be alert and able to use her limbs we will often use a product called Neo Calglucon, a liquid calcium product made for human babies (it can be purchased with a prescription from any local drug store) to help restore her calcium balance. This quickly absorbed calcium source is metabolized into a deficient female chameleon's body and rapidly deposited where it is most needed. Usually terribly deficient animals will also have severe muscle tremors and difficulty grasping anything, these are both signs of advanced metabolic bone disease. Female chameleons with these symptoms are so depleted of calcium that they usually become egg bound and unable to lay their eggs. This condition is usually fatal when it has progressed this far.

Stress

Stress when combined with the improper environment is probably the number one reason why chameleons do not flourish in captivity. It is not an illness, but the result of factors caused from illness or other outside sources that culminates in the animal becoming stressed and unable to function within its given parameters. There are many possible causes of stress that can be eliminated from the captive chameleon's environment and when removed will make life much easier for these animals. It is believed that there are high levels of stress that on a long-term basis are health hazards, and there are also levels of nonlife-threatening stresses that are normal. I will list but a few of the more usual causes of stress below. After reading the following list the reader will get an overall idea of the underlying causes of stress.

1. Chameleons do not like to socialize with

other chameleons except when breeding. Animals forced to live in close proximity to other chameleons or reptiles will often stress and live a suboptimal life under these conditions. If it is absolutely necessary to keep chameleons together then it is essential to offer enough room for them to escape from the immediate vicinity of another animal. We keep large colonies of chameleons in our greenhouses and have noticed that when given the psychological benefit of space, these animals will live quite amicably together as long as they know they can escape. At times we find animals close to each other in the same bush and then on a following day these same chameleons will be several yards away from each other.

2. Gravid females especially dislike being near another chameleon and particularly another male of their own species. Gravid females that are being pursued by amorous males will be very stressed and often become egg bound and unable to lay their eggs in a safe refuge. These animals often die as a result.

3. Incorrect shipping, both locally and internationally, have profound influences on chameleons. Chameleons must always be shipped individually in their own container or in a cloth bag suspended within the outer shipping container. Animals shipped either together or packed individually in bags but then piled upon one another usually are badly stressed and heavy losses can occur as a result. We prefer shipping animals packed in their own small enclosure with a perch firmly attached inside for them to grasp during shipment. The use of cloth bags is also good as long as plenty of space is allowed around the enclosed animal and it is not tightly packed or placed in a pile but rather suspended from a fixture specially built inside of the shipping container. Chameleons should always be thoroughly hydrated just prior to packing them for shipment.

4. Temperatures outside of the comfort ranges of each species often result in terrible stress problems that can result in permanent brain and organ damage or other neurological problems or even death. Overheating appears to be much more stressful than a drop of temperature to most species. Freezing temperatures are only tolerated by a few species and in these cases, temperatures do not reach severe freezing for long periods of several hours. During the winter, international shipments from Africa or Madagascar passing through Europe before arriving in the United States are often exposed to severe cold which results in animals that either arrive dead or that will die later from kidney and other organ damage.

5. Parasites take a heavy toll on chameleons and create unhealthy conditions that cause considerable stress. If parasites are not eliminated or at least controlled, the resultant stress usually will kill the parasitized animal. If the parasite load is great and the animals are treated by an inexperienced person, the treatment along with the dying parasites will also cause tremendous stress and oftentimes death. It always pays to use a competent veterinarian or private breeder with experience when it comes to deparasitization of animals.

6. Even animals that are kept separate from each other but that can view another animal in close proximity can become stressed. A lot of animals will live peacefully and will not exhibit stress from this closeness, as long as they have their own environment intact and they know it will not be invaded. Other individuals simply do not tolerate another visible animal of their own species or a completely different species within their area. Usually this is simple to remedy by placing a visual barrier between the cages.

7. Keeping a captive chameleon in an enclosure without plants to hide in is cruel. These animals have developed close relationships with their surrounding floral biota over the eon of time and must be provided with cover in order to feel at ease. Plastic plants or those made of silk are a last-ditch effort to provide these animals with refuge. A chameleon living in an environment that does not support living, healthy plant life is liv-

ing in hell! Use living plants as your indicator that you are providing a healthful environment for your chameleons.

8. Overhandling and forcing a chameleon to constantly fire up its brilliant defensive coloration is only asking for this animal to become stressed and ill. Handle your animals with the attitude that they are living, breathing creatures adapted to hiding and being left alone in the jungle. These animals are not toys of modern life in the city, useful for showing off to friends and at social events. Treat them with respect and they will reward you with long life and unbounded wonderment.

The following signs of stress are only the more prominent ones and the competent chameleon keeper will learn to recognize these and others in the individual animals in their care.

1. Upper-respiratory illness is often a direct result of a chameleon becoming stressed from a wide assortment of causes. Although usually bacterial in origin, this condition can be traced to a stressful event within the previous two weeks of the sick chameleon's life. Upper-respiratory illness manifests itself by a watery discharge or a thick mucus discharge from the nose or mouth. Heavy breathing with difficulty is also a sure sign of this condition. Sometimes merely allowing the animal to live in a peaceful environment away from any other outside disturbance will result in the abatement of all symptoms of upper-respiratory illness. Usually the condition requires immediate attention in order to save the animal's life. If the illness grows progressively worse in symptoms over a couple of days immediate treatment is absolutely essential! In this case a bacterial agent is usually the culprit and needs to be identified and destroyed with the use of an antibiotic. This involves advanced medical procedures correctly employed and should be done under the care of a good reptilian veterinarian if possible. The shotgun approach of administering antibiotics sometimes works well and at other times causes problems that have long-term effects on the animal's health. This is not a condi-

tion to be taken lightly and should be treated aggressively and by a person well versed in this field.

2. Dark, unusual coloration not normally used by the particular animal is a sure indication that something is not right in its environment. This could be a result from some outside factor such as too much heat or an offending dog or bird that has gotten too close for comfort. In these instances the animal will resume normal coloration after the offenders have left the area. When an animal stays dark and doesn't resume its proper color range concern is warranted by the keeper. A thorough investigation should be taken and a determination of the cause of the psychological or physiological condition should be assessed.

3. A sudden cessation in eating is often a cause for alarm to the chameleon keeper. Animals that go off their food either are bored with the particular items being offered and need a change of food items or may have a more serious problem lurking. A chameleon that is healthy and that has been eating is completely different from the recently imported, emaciated specimen that needs nourishment in order to survive. Parasites migrating within the body of a stressed lizard often result in it going off of its food. Breeding males will also go off of feeding for several days at a time and will not usually exhibit any other signs of stress and should not cause alarm to the keeper. A close eye on the chameleon that is not eating usually reveals the reason for this situation. If this cannot be ascertained then a more experienced person should be questioned and preferably should view the animal in its environment.

4. A sleepy animal that keeps its eyes closed and stays this way during normal hours of activity is suspect of being stressed. Often the stressor is an external one such as a recent change in the animal's environment. Check to see if the light level has changed in the animal's area recently or another incidental change has taken place. Sometimes a sleepy animal is a very pregnant animal

and just needs to rest shortly before giving birth or laying eggs.

Parasites

Worms

Much has been said of parasites in this book. They are a constant threat to the health and well-being of all chameleons. In nature, chameleons seem to exist with these lower life forms and carry out their lives walking the narrow line between life and death with an internal load of various types of worms and protozoans. It probably would make a very interesting study for a student of herpetology, to determine just how much the wild-living chameleons are effected by these parasite loads. It has been recorded in some species of South African chameleons that there are periods of the year when the population is heavily parasitized and at other times the animals are practically free of worms. This interesting phenomenon seems to also occur in Madagascan animals and there are times of the year when imported animals seem much less parasitized then at other times. We wonder if this is a result of a natural jungle remedy such as insects eating a certain plant and then passing its deparasitizing effects onto the chameleon that eats those gut-loaded insects? Animals that are imported during the Madagascan winter, a time of cooler and drier environmental conditions are usually much less parasitized then animals shipped during the wetter and warmer seasons. This relationship between parasites and seasons might also be connected to stress factors on the animals who are exposed to drier times without food and water.

Figure 5.6: Deceased male *C. pardalis*—blue morph with parasites.

Any chameleon that has been imported from a foreign source and that has not been treated at least twice for parasites is not a good candidate for the reader to consider for their own collection. Even foreign, farm-raised animals can have parasites as these are usually fed on wild insects and are exposed to areas with biting insects that can spread filarians to them. Insects are usually the main vectors (spreaders) of worm parasites but contact with infected fecal material can also be a serious infection site for some species of worms. Animals that are not checked beforehand and deemed parasite free should not be placed nearby or with other chameleons that are free of parasites. We know of instances where infected animals were brought into collections that had parasite free animals and shortly thereafter these animals were infected and some were lost as a result. Never, never introduce animals that are suspect in any way to an established collection, this act often results in grief to the collector and death to the chameleons. There are companies that sell deparasitized, imported chameleons and they have made every effort to make sure that this is the case but occasionally a parasite sneaks through the process of deparasitization and it is always a good idea to quarantine new animals and recheck them prior to introduction to the area that might house other specimens. This same advice holds for the individual with only one animal. A simple fecal check is usually inexpensive at a local veterinarians and can offer a lot of peace of mind to the new owner. I will add here that every species of internal parasite that could possibly infect a chameleon cannot be detected by examination of the feces alone. If the owner or his veterinarian suspects filarians for instance, then blood work will also have to be run on the chameleon to be on the safe side.

There are species of parasites that will not respond to most medications and that require special treatments or that cannot be treated at all. Some of these wormlike creatures are not worms at all but very primitive members of the spider family that burrow through tissue and often lodge themselves in the lungs of reptiles. We have had very few animals infected with these but they do exist and it is a chance that one takes with wild-caught or foreign farm-raised animals.

It is always prudent to allow an animal that needs to be deparasitized a few days to adjust to its new environment before attempting to worm or treat it for protozoans. This will give the chameleon a chance to eat and drink before the medication is administered.

I feel strongly that all imported chameleons need to be treated prophylactically for common worm parasites as well as flagellates. Even animals that are checked and found to have very low numbers of parasites should be treated as these numbers can explode into large loads fairly quickly. If the reader has obtained a new chameleon that has been imported and not deparasitized and he wishes to perform this risky treatment himself then my advice is to at least take a fecal to a veterinarian and have the doctor check for specific parasites and numbers. As much fecal material should be taken as is possible to collect and even feces that have accumulated over several days will be useful to the veterinarian. It really is better to take the fecal sample in to the veterinarian without the animal, stress from the packing and unpacking as well as the trip can be harmful especially to a new animal. If the veterinarian determines that the animal has a heavy parasite load and needs professional management then it will be necessary to take the animal to the veterinarian post haste. Every effort should be made to transfer the new chameleon as comfortably and free of stress as possible.

For the advanced chameleon keeper or the stubborn do-it-yourselfer without experience (I know you exist and will need the following information) the following medical advice has been formulated by our veterinarians experienced with reptiles. If it is absolutely impossible for the reader to find a chameleon-experienced veterinarian, then you must take the bull by the horns and deparasitize your animal(s) yourself. Because chameleons are so prone to having worms, it is a good idea to check them on a yearly basis for parasites and treat when needed.

The drug of choice for deworming chameleons as well as other reptiles is 10 percent Fenbendazole paste usually used for worming horses and other cattle. The brand name most often associated with this drug is Panacur and can be bought over the counter in most feed stores and other businesses catering to the horse and cattle rancher. Panacur will effectively treat most, if not all, roundworms such as nematodes and ascarids. It is not effective against flatworms also known as tapeworms and blood-born filarial species. For tapeworms the recommended vermifuge is Praziquantel whose most recognized brand name is Droncit. There are other medications that will also work but Droncit has been effective so we have not needed to use others and cannot offer any comment as to their effectiveness. Droncit in the hands of a person who is inexperienced in its use for chameleons is a very dangerous drug. It should only be used when nothing else is possible and only in the hands of an experienced person.

Blood-born worms are quite resistant to most vermifuges and we have only found one drug useful in eradication of these killers. The drug Ivermectin has been a Godsend in ridding most animals infested with microfilarial worms. This drug is extremely dangerous when overdosed and should only be used by persons who have an intimate knowledge of its usage. Even very tiny overdoses have resulted in the slow deaths of animals.

Dosage Chart for Ivermectin (Ivomec)

To dilute the Ivomec: mix 0.1 cc of 1 percent (full strength = 10 mg/ml) Ivomec with 0.9 cc of injectable propylene glycol, sterile water or saline solution.

This gives a solution of 0.1 percent = 1 mg/ml Ivomec. The dose is 0.2 mg/kg body weight. The drug can be administered by injection into the shoulder or preferably by oral route.

WEIGHT OF CHAMELEON

grams	Dose (dilute) Ivomec
50	.01 ml
75	.015 ml
100	.02 ml
125	.03 ml
150	.03 ml
175	.04 ml
200	.04 ml

grams	Dose (dilute) Ivomec
250	.05 ml
300	.06 ml
350	.07 ml
400	.08 ml
450	.10 ml

Protozoans

After considering the above worm parasites we now must focus our attention on the second and equally important group of parasites in chameleons—the protozoans. Wild-caught chameleons usually harbor a vast array of small protozoans generally grouped under the flagellates. These microscopic little devils can devastate a chameleon's intestinal tract in short order once they overpopulate the gut due to stress and other biological factors which trigger an increase in their numbers. Normally a chameleon lives with most flagellates quite harmoniously and there isn't much of a problem. In fact, it is sometimes not necessary to treat for them at all. However, we generally do treat prophylactically as a pre-

Figure 5.7: Oral administration of drug to a male *C. Globifer*.

Figure 5.8: Oral administration to a female *C. parsonii*.

cautionary measure in newly imported animals, since we have learned from experience that by treating we have far less problems than if we don't treat. The drug of choice for this treatment is Metronidazole generally known by the brand name Flagyl. It should be noted that this drug is also a strong antibiotic and when overdosed it can cause severe gastric distress in a susceptible animal. The drug is quite capable of wiping out all of the beneficial intestinal bacteria that the chameleon needs for digestion and the manufacture of certain nutrients and other natural defense mechanisms. Flagyl is available from some veterinarians once they are convinced that the user understands its usage well. This is a good place to initiate deparasitization and it should be a part of the initial cleaning regime.

We prefer to administer both Panacur and Flagyl at the same time. We do not advise doing the same with Ivermectin or other drugs mentioned. Some people prefer to dose all drugs separately, a day apart, and this also works well if the administrator will keep careful track of the dates and dosages. Both drugs are administered orally with an oral medication syringe and not with an injection syringe with a needle on it. Dosage rates can be found below for the above drugs.

It is important to note that usually a course of treatment involves two treatments of the two drugs, however, a fecal check two weeks after the last treatment might reveal that the animal still has parasites and another course will have to be given until the final check reveals no parasites. On very rare occasions we have had worm species that resisted Panacur treatment and we had to use other vermifuges. If this happens to you it would be wise to consult a veterinarian that has had experience in these matters.

For your convenience, the following table of medication dosages is provided. Note the strengths of each drug used, as they come in different strengths and the dosages will need to be adjusted accordingly. To make Panacur paste easier to draw into a syringe, it can be mixed with equal parts of water. If this medication is diluted, the dose amounts below must be doubled. It is important to remember to fully hydrate chameleons before any treatments, an hour-long shower is desirable.

Full-strength Dosages for Panacur and Flagyl

Weight	Panacur	Flagyl
50 grams	.05 ccs	.20 ccs
75 grams	.07 ccs	.28 ccs
100 grams	.10 ccs	.40 ccs
125 grams	.12 ccs	.48 ccs
150 grams	.15 ccs	.60 ccs
175 grams	.17 ccs	.68 ccs
200 grams	.20 ccs	.80 ccs

Panacur should be given by placing the tip of the syringe with the proper dose amount into the back of the throat. After dispensing, the animal should be allowed to swallow the medication prior to giving any further dosages. Panacur should be given once and then again in 7 days to effectively interrupt the life cycle of most worm species.

Flagyl has a more controversial treatment schedule. It is also administered orally in the same manner as Panacur. The duration of the treatment is often debated among veterinarians. Some prefer to give a single dose and repeat it in two weeks. Others feel that in some reptiles such as chameleons the treatment should be given once and then again in 7 days. We usually go with the latter line of treatment and have found it works well for us.

Using the above dose chart it is important to note that if the chameleon you are treating is smaller than 50 grams, give only a small drop of each drug to the chameleon at the prescribed times. If the chameleon is larger than 200 grams, use the chart to figure a higher dosage rate. If a chameleon is between weights on the chart, go to the next highest dosage. These drugs are very safe when dosed within range, and have little to no side effects if used as directed. It is important that you know the correct weight of the chameleon before you attempt to use this chart.

Sick Chameleons in General

Normally when a chameleon has an infection or a heavy parasite load, it will probably have stopped drinking and eating and will have become thin. Obviously this presents a life-threatening condition if not assisted by the keeper immediately. In this condition, we generally have had a positive response by using the carbo-

hydrate and electrolyte booster Emeraid 1 and wouldn't be caught dead without it in our chameleon first aid kit. If the chameleon is drinking on its own and appears to be well hydrated, we do not administer this product. If the animal is not drinking and eating adequately we begin treatment with Emeraid 1 immediately. If we cannot entice the chameleon to drink the Emeraid 1 by placing it at first in small amounts into its opened mouth we will convert over to the use of Lactated-Ringers solution with 5 percent dextrose injected under the skin in amounts that will make the chameleon appear as though it is well hydrated. This solution has saved many very sick animals for us and other owners who know how and when to use it.

Emeraid 1 must be obtained from a veterinarian, as the product is not sold to the public. Normally we have found veterinarians quite willing to stock us up on this product as a first aid device in treating our sick animals. We give Emeraid 1 (to animals not eating or drinking) for the first week, twice a day, and then only once a day for the next week. We also offer water by sprinkling it over the animal in a rain-like manner once a day. If the chameleon begins to take the water but not in sufficient amounts for complete hydration we continue the Emeraid for a third week. After this period of time we offer the Emeraid every other day until the chameleon eats and drinks on its own. Once mixed, Emerald 1 is good for 24 hours so only mix up what is needed at one time.

Administering Medications

Special care should be taken when giving either oral or injectable medications to chameleons. A normally docile animal can become violent and bite when forced into accepting any medication. It is usually advisable that two people adept at handling an unruly animal be used when giving medication to a chameleon. One person should concentrate on holding and, when needed, restraining the animal, and the other should focus on giving the injection or oral medication as quickly and painlessly as possible.

If the animal must be injected and there is only one handler to perform the task, the easiest and least stressful method to employ is to wrap the animal in a hand towel and only expose the area to be injected (usually the shoulder region). After the injection the rumpled chameleon will have calmed down and the towel can be unwrapped and the animal placed back into its enclosure.

Oral administration by one person usually is much easier and it is often possible to leave the chameleon in its enclosure during treatment unless it cannot be reached or is in an awkward position for treatment. After positioning the animal in a convenient head-on direction, gently place your fingers over the nostril holes at the tip of the snout. Only apply enough pressure to keep the animal from pulling away from your fingers but do not cause the animal any real discomfort. This usually elicits an open-mouth response in all but the sickest or tamest animals. After the mouth is opened sufficiently, introduce a medication syringe and administer the medication. After dosing try to wait for the chameleon to close its mouth before letting its body go. This will allow the medicine to stay inside the mouth and not be expelled by the chameleon.

Sometimes an animal simply will not open its mouth after a lot of cajoling. The next step will be to gently take the animal behind the head and shake it slightly. If this does not work, a gentle repeated tap on the nose may be needed. As a last resort, pry the mouth open with the tip of a dull butter knife or other instrument or a gentler alternative is to pull gently on the gular area, which is the flap of skin under the throat. Be especially careful in pulling on this, as the skin on the gular can rip or the inner tissue can be torn and cause even more problems.

The following two injectable antibiotics have proven themselves to be the most useful for bacterial infections in chameleons. Their use should not be undertaken by the inexperienced or the fainthearted. Both Baytril and Amikacin are prescription drugs and can only be purchased through a veterinarian. It would be wise to use these drugs under the supervision of the veterinarian that will provide these to the collector.

Figure 5.9: Medication injection into the shoulder of a male *C. globifer.*

Figure 5.10: Female *C. verrucosus* with a severe skin tourniquet causing loss of foot.

This makes a 5 mg/ml solution, the dose is 0.45 mg/kg body weight.

WEIGHT OF CHAMELEON

grams	diluted	full strength
500	.02 ml	0
750	.03 ml	0
1000	.05 ml	0
1250	.06 ml	0
1500	.07 ml	0
1750	.08 ml	0.01 ml
2000	.09 ml	0.01 ml
2500	.1 ml	0.01 ml
3000	.14 ml	0.015 ml
3500	.16 ml	0.02 ml
4000	.18 ml	0.02 ml
4500	.2 ml	0.02 ml
5000	.23 ml	0.03 ml

Dosage Chart for Amikacin

To dilute: mix 0.1 cc of 50 mg/ml (full strength) Amikacin with 0.9 cc of sterile water.

Dosage Chart for Baytril

Use Baytril 22.7 mg/ml, dose at 7.5 mg/kg body weight.

WEIGHT OF CHAMELEON

grams	dose
500	.015 ml
750	.02 ml
1000	.03 ml
1250	.04 ml
1500	.05 ml
1750	.06 ml
2000	.07 ml
2500	.09 ml
3000	.1 ml
3500	.12 ml
4000	.14 ml
4500	
5000	

** If unable to find a chameleon-experienced veterinarian, contact Scott Stahl, D.V.M. at Pender Veterinary Clinic, 4001 Legato Road, Fairfax, VA 22033 (703) 591-3304. For a consultation fee, Dr. Stahl is open to helping you with your chameleon's particular problems.

6

Breeding Chameleons

After having kept chameleons a while, most people have caught the fever of maintaining and studying these fascinating animals and will usually follow the natural progression and will want to breed their animals. The challenge of keeping and finally breeding these animals under captive conditions is both fascinating and a worthwhile objective and can be accomplished if the keeper has done his homework and knows his animals well.

Most acclimated chameleons that have adapted to our seasonal changes for at least a year will choose to mate in our springtime (North America). There are some species that are not particular about a breeding season and these will mate throughout the year. In those species, it is generally the rule that these are the multiple-clutch species where the females either lay or give birth more than once a year. An example would be the panther chameleon, *Chamaeleo pardalis*, which can lay up to 4 clutches of around 20–30

Figure 6.1: Receptive mating of a female *C. pardalis* red morph.
Photo: David Adamson

eggs per clutch per year. These females mature and breed at an early age and are subsequently gravid for the rest of their reproductive lives. Normally a female chameleon from one of the more productive species will retain active sperm and will autofertilize more than one clutch of eggs so that it is possible to have an impregnated female lay several clutches of fertile eggs without being exposed to a male for many months. In those species such as Parson's chameleon, *C. parsonii*, the females only lay eggs once a year and usually need to be fertilized every year in order to produce viable eggs.

A gravid female chameleon does not like to be in the proximity of an amorous male and will usually exhibit gravid coloration which is different from what she normally displays. This coloration will announce to the males that she does not want anything to do with them. Even when these females exhibit this defensive pattern, some males will try to mount them and it is advisable to remove a gravid female after mating has taken place so that she does not become overly stressed.

Actual mating of captive animals is accomplished after the correct season and physical condition of the animals have been established. Breeding animals need to be in healthy condition, well fed and filled out. A thin, undernourished animal might mate but the resultant number and health of the offspring often reflect the malnourishment of the female. It is important to note that overly nourished animals should also not be bred, especially the females. When a female chameleon is too fat she becomes an egg-

Figure 6.2: Nonreceptive female *C. pardalis.*

producing factory that often overloads with an inordinate amount of fertile, growing eggs within her body. We have seen young, overweight female chameleons that have been bred and have developed so many eggs within their bodies that they were unable to expel them when the time came. The eggs then became overdue and the females' bodies become toxic and they died. Females that are full of eggs usually do not have much room for food intake and this can also be a problem with an overly productive female. Egg production takes a lot out of the female's system and she must be adequately nourished with proper protein and balanced mineral levels which enable her to produce viable eggs that in turn develop into strong healthy young. During the time of internal egg development a female should be fed on high-quality, egg-bearing female crickets that have been well mineralized with dusting and gutloading. These insects contain hundreds of eggs which are of themselves very nutritious and contain concentrated lipids, proteins and other nutrients that will act as a nutritional booster to the gravid female chameleon. It is important to remember that the gravid female will most likely go off her food after her body becomes so engorged with eggs that she no longer has any room for food. It is important to get good concentrated nutrition into her during the initial period shortly after breeding has taken place. Normally a female will deposit her eggs approximately 50–70 days after mating. Some species will vary from this time period. There is a difference between overfeeding a female at this time and giving her adequate but concentrated nutrition. We recommend feeding at least

1, 2 or more egg-bearing crickets to a gravid female every day.

If the chameleon breeder has kept his animals separated during the year and introduces them together during the mating season, the animals usually will not have much hesitation when it comes to the actual act of copulation. We usually place the female in the male's environment and stand by in case there are any signs of aggression from either side. Breeding of chameleons usually involves a certain amount of forcefulness on the male's behalf and it has been likened to outright rape by more than one person. The normal sequence usually goes as follows: the female is introduced into the male's enclosure. She will usually look a little uneasy and may not be very friendly toward the male, but she may not pay any attention to him either. The male on the other hand will begin an immediate display of brightened colors, head wagging or bobbing and will usually proceed toward the female's position. Upon reaching the female he will waste no time on formalities and will usually grab her by the tail or a leg and will pull her struggling body toward him. Once she is in the proper place he will mount her and she will usually submit and hold still during the mating act. The time period for mating can vary from a few minutes to more than an hour and the animals should not be disturbed during this time. After the mating has taken place, the pair will pull apart and the female will usually try to escape from the vicinity of the male. Sometimes the female will stay near the male and show no hostility toward him. We usually remove the female to her own enclosure and she will start exhibiting gravid coloration within a day or so of the mating. If the female does not show gravid coloration she might not have been impregnated and the mating should be retried. If she has indeed been fertilized on the first breeding and just hasn't colored up with gravid color yet, she will not be at all receptive to the excited male and will fend him off when he tries to mate with her.

Sometimes breeding does not go as outlined above and the animals will take their sweet time before mating. If breeding has not commenced within 1 hour after placing the female with the male, remove the female, and try again in a week. Often this break between will peak the male's interest and the next meeting will be more fruitful.

Figure 6.4: Female *C. parsonii* digging in a depository.
Photo: Les Brigham

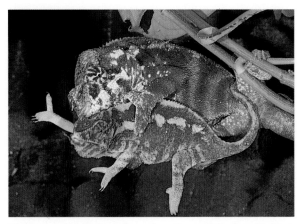

Figure 6.3: Violent mating of a *C. pardalis* female by a male—red morph.

If you are intending to try to breed your animals, and I hope you are, then please try to purchase only unrelated animals to start with. If everybody does this it will insure the future gene pool of all species currently kept in captivity. Some species are represented by very small gene pools and extra effort must be made to keep these animals genetically divergent and pure to avoid genetic depression and hybridization. Breeding only the strongest and healthiest chameleons will also add to the future strength of the gene pool.

Gravid Female Detection

I mentioned earlier that the newly gravid female will exhibit a different coloration than normal after insemination has occurred. There are other characteristics that also help the breeder to determine whether or not his female animal is gravid.

About 3–4 weeks into a pregnancy a female chameleon will have noticeably grown in girth. If the breeder will take a suspected female into his hand and gently palpate (pressing the abdominal wall between 2 opposing fingers in a massaging motion) the underbelly region it will be possible to feel developing eggs through the body wall. Press gently in a circular motion. If the female is far enough along, small eggs the

size of jelly beans will be felt. If the female is very near to the time for deposition of her eggs the actual outline of the eggs closest to the abdominal wall can be seen as lumps on the outside outline of the body. These lumpy females are often called marble bags by some breeders.

After a female has deposited her eggs (see Gravid Female Enclosures) it will be safe to reintroduce her to a male usually 2 weeks after egg laying. Normally a female has had time to replenish her body with nutrients and fat deposits and is ready to be bred again. If the female still seems too thin and stressed from the previous egg laying or live birth then wait until she returns to her normal self before continuing with this step. The breeder can assist the post-egglaying female by bolstering her diet with well-mineralized female crickets that are full of eggs. This added nutrition really helps weakened females through this period. Old female chameleons seem to have the hardest time with post-egglaying depression and will need to be watched carefully.

Breeding a female shortly after egglaying, if possible, will ensure that future clutches of eggs will have enough sperm to fertilize them. If sufficient sperm is not stored by a female chameleon ensuing clutches might be totally or partially sterile and it would be a shame to waste this female's eggs needlessly. When a female chameleon becomes mature enough to breed, it is her mission in life to be constantly gravid and reproduce her kind. It is true that by carrying out this natural plan she will shorten her life span and will usually burn out long before a male of the same species does. Chameleons that bear several clutches per year are susceptible to short lives and this pattern can be somewhat delayed by breeding females only once or twice per year. We know people who have tried this method with limited success. Usually the female that has been bred only once has been fertilized well enough that she will continue having eggs in decreasing viability up to the point of death. One method that seems to work at slowing down a female's urge to lay eggs is to give her a cooling-off period after her second or third laying. This is merely a time of about 2 months when the temperatures are reduced into the lower sixties during the nighttime and rises only into the lower seventies Fahrenheit during the day. We have noticed that gravid females exposed to lower temperatures will lose their gravid coloration and seem to delay any further egg development until temperatures rise again.

A female showing problems with labor must be assisted if her life is to be saved and the eggs rescued before they become toxic in her body. Labor distress is usually easily identifiable and steps need to be taken immediately to correct the situation. When the female chameleon is ready to lay her eggs she will have dug a hole usually as long as she is and will deposit the eggs in it somewhat effortlessly. Usually this process goes smoothly but once in a while in very young or very old females, or animals with inadequate blood calcium levels, this process goes wrong. The distressed female will exhibit signs of labor distress by hanging from a limb by her front legs, usually with her head back and mouth open (as if she were imitating a wolf howling at the moon) at this stage she is in early distress. If she is digging in several locations and does not seem happy with any of these, simply moving her to a trash can depository with a deep bed of potting soil and a hiding plant might take care of the problem and she will dig and deposit her load of eggs. If this method does not work or she is already in a trash can and in distress then she must receive immediate medical treatment.

We keep as part of our chameleon medical emergency kit the injectable medication Oxytocin, which is the drug of choice for inducing labor in people as well as animals. This drug is obtainable through a veterinarian and is an absolute lifesaver for female animals unable to deliver eggs or babies normally. The drug, when given at the proper rate, is safe and effective. Usually a female will start delivery within a few minutes to an hour after Oxytocin has been administered by injection. The drug is injected intramuscularly at the upper base of the tail at the rate of .05 international units per 70 grams of body weight. This dosage is used on smaller animals and is increased for larger animals such as an adult Parson's chameleon which would receive up to 0.1 international units of Oxytocin. We never use more than this amount on any animal. Occasionally we have an animal that will expel only part of her eggs and will retain the rest. In this case we will redose with the Oxytocin in an effort to clean her out. This second dose is administered after one and a half hours from the time the first injection was given and only when there has not been any eggs laid or only a couple of eggs have been expelled. Sometimes a drug-induced female will just have a slow labor and will drop eggs over a period of an hour and a half but continues laying periodically. In this case we do not inject a second time with the Oxytocin and will allow her to keep laying at a reduced speed. We only inject Oxytocin twice, if too many doses are employed the oviduct can become sticky and it will not be possible for the eggs to pass through it. We have experimented with several dosages of Oxytocin and find that it is better to give a higher dose than what is used on other types of animals in order to induce the female chameleon to lay all of her eggs simultaneously. On rare occasions we have experienced a female that will lay an

Figure 6.5: Female *C. pardalis* with a prolapse due to egg binding.

egg on the surface of the potting mix in the depository cage without digging a proper hole for deposition. In this case we will also induce labor by using the Oxytocin, as this female is also in jeopardy of not expelling all of her eggs.

Oxytocin is highly unstable when not kept at a very cool temperature. This should be kept in mind at all times and only Oxytocin that has been constantly kept refrigerated should be used. Likewise when injecting a chameleon with this drug it should first be warmed to room temperature before injecting, as very cold Oxytocin is painful when injected. The brief time taken to bring it to room temperature will not effect the drug's potency at all.

Every so often we have a female that requires Oxytocin treatment but still is unable to dispel her eggs. Usually this female dies and upon

Figure 6.6: Prolapse female with egg binding and ovary wrap necropsy

dissection it is found that she has a contortion of the oviduct that did not allow passage of the eggs and it was impossible for her to lay. With experience we now recognize this problem ahead of the females imminent death and will sacrifice the female and rescue the eggs before they also die. This is a very hard decision to make but a necessary one nevertheless. If the female has retained the eggs for a long time and then dies, the chances of these eggs surviving is practically nil.

Incubation of Eggs

Once a female has deposited her eggs and has refilled the nesting material over them, it is time to remove the eggs for safe incubation. It should be noted that it is always extremely important to allow the female to complete the act of burying her eggs and then leaving them. If this advice is ignored and the eggs are taken before the entire burying process has been completed, the female will often continue to repeat the whole process over and over again. A female chameleon's brain does not seem to comprehend that the eggs are missing and she should forget the matter. If I have several females laying at the same time I will mark the nest site of each one so that I do not forget where the female buried her eggs. I use a piece of wire or small twig pushed into the potting soil right next to the spot where I observe her depositing her eggs.

Remove the newly laid eggs by digging them up carefully and place them into a prepared Tupperware or similar plastic container with a sealable lid. To prepare the incubation chamber prior to placing the eggs in it we fill the container halfway with dampened vermiculite into which we place the eggs. Each egg is buried halfway along its side axis with the top side being exposed for observation. We place the eggs in rows so that they don't touch each other and so that water can be added to dry vermiculite around the eggs without soaking the eggs. Eggs that do fungus after some incubation time are infertile and should be removed. Fungus will not generally attack a fertile, live embryo. After all of the eggs are in place we seal the lid so ants or other insects and dry air cannot enter the incubation chamber and then place the container in an area that we know will maintain the correct temperature over the period of incubation that is appropriate for the particular species being incubated. We do check the eggs on a weekly basis for any fungus growth or spoiling.

Proper mixing of the vermiculite with water prior to placing the eggs in it will assure that the eggs get a good start with humidity. It is very easy to hydrate the vermiculite by simply spraying the dried material with an atomizer or other sprayer device until the vermiculite becomes saturated and feels damp to the touch. Mix the material while spraying it to assure even penetration of the water throughout. Too much moisture is not beneficial to the developing embryos

Figure 6.7: Squeeze testing vermiculite.

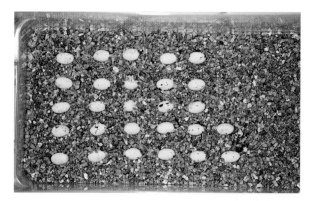

Figure 6.8: *C. pardalis* eggs sweating before hatching.

and too little is just as bad. The proper level of moisture can be ascertained by squeezing a small amount of the soaked material between the fingers. If more than a few drops of water appear from the soaked vermiculite then it will be too wet for incubation and additional dry material will need to be mixed into the damp material. It may take a few attempts to blend the proper ratio of water to vermiculite but after this the reader will find the process quite simple to repeat. Keep this consistency until close to hatching time (see specific species for triggering spring simulations). After the recommended incubation at this level of moisture in the vermiculite, add more water so that when the vermiculite is pinched, water runs down your arm, but not so much that the eggs are covered with water. This will simulate a spring rainy season. The eggs will swell with moisture allowing the shell to thin so the baby can break out more easily. The extra water also acts as a sign which says spring is here, conditions are right for hatching and food is plentiful.

When placing the eggs in the incubation container they should have a surrounding border of vermiculite (see figure) on the outside edge. This will allow for the adding of water if the eggs should dent and become dehydrated during the long incubation period. Mist the edges of the tub, and the water will wick through the rest of the medium. You can always add more water in a few days. If dehydrated eggs don't pop back into shape after rewetting the vermiculite, test for moisture again. If this is correct, do not add any more water. Simply bury the eggs further

into the vermiculite where more of their surface will be in contact with the medium and check again in a few days. If the eggs are viable and have not been allowed to dry for too long they will return to their original state.

Never allow any water drops to collect on the lid of the container as the drops may drown the eggs. Once the eggs are inside the container, do not wash them off. The dirt will not hurt the eggs if it is not removed completely, but spraying water on them directly may drown them.

It should also be remembered that after the first week of incubation the eggs have already started to develop inside and they should only be handled by a very careful person who will not drop, shake or bump the incubation container. Even handling the eggs can be dangerous for the embryo forming inside. If an egg that is developing is rolled over or in some way jostled it can separate the embryo from its proper attachment in the egg and it will die. A precautionary measure often used is to dot the very topside of the exposed part of the egg with a nontoxic felt marker. Should you accidentally drop the egg, it will have a better chance of survival if it is placed back in its original position. You will notice that in the egg incubation sections that will follow, the temperature range is consistently kept at 68–74°F. This temperature range simulates that range found in nature. Experiments were conducted by probing the earth 6–12 inches underground over a 1-year period, the temperature was consistently 68–74°F. These experiments took place in the desert and in a subtropical area with like results.

7

Popular Species and Their Environments

This chapter is intended as a brief overview of the various species that the chameleon keeper might have available to him. Many of the species included are frequently available from importers, pet stores and captive breeding programs. When I wrote the first draft of this manuscript three years ago, the following species were being imported regularly. In June of 1995 some of these same animals were nearly impossible to find in the pet trade and will probably only be available in the near future from captive breeders. This is how fast changes in the animal trade can take place. Madagascar has recently initiated a new regulation that currently only allows four species of *Chamaeleo* to be captured and exported. This law does encourage captive breeding for export purposes by Malagasy exporters and hopefully this will take place. Other countries are looking at similar regulations and will shortly stop the export of wild-caught animals. In some cases due to wars, famines and other natural events several species have disappeared from trade altogether.

The following information is furnished as a result of brainstorming with other breeders around the world. I have tried to provide as accurate a record of the species and their requirements as possible. The information has been hard won in many instances by other breeders, as well as ourselves, and if followed should be useful to the reader. In some instances the chameleon keeper should take into account that some of the habitat and other requirements are broadly interpreted and will have to be adjusted to their own needs and requirements while at the same time providing the animals with the best conditions possible. It should be remembered that there is more than one way to successfully keep and breed these lizards as long as the overall conditions are correct. Many husbandry techniques are purely experimental at this time, and have been included because they have been proven in the hands of competent breeders. I have intentionally deleted some experimental techniques that have not been tested for a long enough period prior to this book being published.

Moderation is perhaps the best word to describe the dilemma of keeping certain species of chameleons in climatic areas where they would never occur naturally. An example would be the keeping of a montane species such as the four-horned chameleon, *C. quadricornis*, in a desert environment such as one would find in Palm Springs, California; a hot, dry and totally inhospitable place for such a species and without an artificial habitat provided by an attentive keeper this climate would mean certain death as well. There are several breeders of this species who live in the California desert regions and have altered their animals' living environments enough that they are thriving and reproducing. The key for these breeders has been to educate themselves regarding the geographical areas and habitat requirements for each species kept and to develop husbandry techniques that have adapted their animals to living in the desert with tolerance of modified desert conditions. If I have learned one thing it is that chameleons are very adaptable given time and patience. These are not animals that tolerate quick environmental changes and need to be acclimated over a period of time. A good example of this is the feral population of Mount Kenya Jackson's chameleons, *C. jacksonii xantholophis*, introduced to several islands in Hawaii many years ago. We recently visited these islands and saw animals living in jungle that is very different from that which they originated. These animals are not exposed to bone-chilling cold in Hawaii as they are during the African winter and yet seem to thrive with only a slight cooling during the Hawaiian seasonal change. Hawaiian nighttime temperatures do not drop nearly as low as they do on Mount Kenya even during the summertime and it appears that this is not needed any longer by the animals that have adapted to the conditions in Hawaii. When Jackson's chameleons, *C. jacksonii*, were imported years ago from the Mount Kenya population they were difficult to keep in captivity unless exposed to a wide temperature fluctuation over a twenty-four-hour period and seasonally. The Hawaiian animals have changed enough through the years through adaptation that this is no longer the case in captives from there. These animals survive much better in captivity than the African imports ever did. Perhaps some of this is a result of the Hawaiian animals being less parasitized and having become used to warmer temperatures that predispose them to living in captive situations.

There seems to be little question that, within reason, chameleons can adapt to varying temperatures, humidity, dryness or other environmental conditions, but the fact remains that they will adjust only in increments and must have some semblance of their natural environment in order to truly thrive. Adaptability does not mean pushing these animals to the extreme limit of their lifestyle. An example would be a species that is known to exist at temperatures from 50–80°F in nature but will tolerate temperatures as high as 95°F and go as low as 35°F on occasion without harm. Even though these animals will take this variance of temperature for a while they will eventually not tolerate the extremes and will become sick and die. Temperatures in the higher range of tolerance will be much easier for the animal to live with if accompanied with proportionally higher humidity levels.

During the heat of a hot summer day a chameleon's skin might become blanched (abnormally light in color) and the animal will open its mouth to pant and relieve itself of internally built up heat. An animal in this condition will need to be offered an area in which to cool down immediately or risk heatstroke. When a chameleon's skin is dark in color and the temperatures are low the lizard could be using a natural method to collect heat rays from the winter sun since dark objects will gather heat from the sun even during very cold temperatures. It would be prudent for the keeper to take this clue and remove the animal from this cold environment and provide it with a more moderate temperature-controlled area. The importance of being observant at all times will enable the chameleon keeper to keep on top of the temperature parameters needed by each of his animals and what they will tolerate given their environment and their behavior.

The following distribution maps will give the reader some idea of the locations where chameleons exist. Many species have spread themselves throughout widely diverse habitats in Madagascar and have acclimated to these amazingly well. In addition to Madagascar I have included maps of South Africa, Cameroon, Tanzania and Yemen.

Madagascar Species

Madagascar has five diverse bio-climatic regions: humid rain forests, arid (deserts), semi-arid, montane and dry. Within these areas the annual rainfall can be between 14–118 inches per year.

1. The east coast is mostly forested and receives 59–118 inches of rainfall per year. Year-round temperatures in the 70–80°F range are common for the northeast portion of the country.

2. The interior escarpment and eastern plateau receives about 59 inches of rainfall per year. This region is only slightly cooler than the northeast coast.

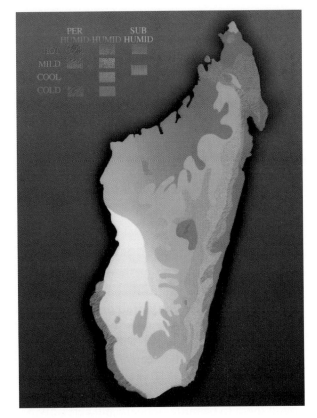

Figure 7.1: Climate map of Madagascar.

Figure 7.2: Male *B. supercilliaris*.   Photo: David Adamson

3. The western plateau may be dry for 6 or more months at a time and then receive 37–59 inches of rainfall over the following 6 months.

4. The western plains can remain dry for 7 or more months, but then receive 20–59 inches over the course of the year. The average temperature in this region of Madagascar is 77–79°F and can occasionally soar up over 104°F.

5. The extreme southwest can remain dry for a year or more, but it can receive up to 14 inches of rainfall per year. The average temperature is 79°F, however, temperatures have been recorded between 104 and 130°F in this region.

Horned Stumptailed Chameleon, *Brookesia supercilliaris*

This species is found in the eastern primary forests of Madagascar. It lives mainly on the forest floor among leaf litter where it is so well camouflaged that it is hard to detect. It is a slow-moving animal that enjoys moderate tem-peratures in the midseventies and shady, damp habitats. It mainly forages on small insects such as species of flies, termites, small isopods and spiders. Like most of the stumptailed chame-leons, it seeks refuge at night by climbing up a plant stalk to a level of several inches or feet. *Brookesia* species usually lay 2 eggs at a time in the leaf litter and will have 2–3 clutches per year. Normal incubation time is surprisingly short and the eggs hatch in 3–4 weeks at a tem-perature of 75°F. Good subjects for the aficio-nado that would like a tabletop vivarium simu-lating a tropical forest environment. We have seen this species kept in pairs in wire-cage ter-rariums with excellent success. The newborn young are extremely small and delicate and re-quire a lot of tedious care in the beginning. These small animals will only consume spring-tails, mites and other extremely small insects and will find even small fruit flies too large to eat at first.

Paddle-nosed or Spiny Chameleon, *Chamaeleo antimena*

This animal comes from the southwestern coast of Madagascar which is hot and often dry with an annual rainfall of 14 inches per year. The species lives in the forest areas that follow along watercourses where it is usually humid and hot. The paddle-nosed chameleon enjoys

Figure 7.3: *C. antimena* female.

Figure 7.5: Male *C. labordi*. See photo of female Figure 1.8 on page 14.

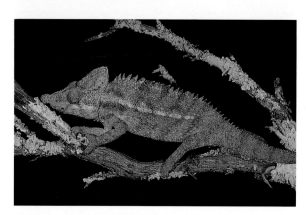

Figure 7.4: Male *C. antimena*.

sunshine and will not live in a dark and cool vivarium for very long. They do best when kept at temperatures between 65 and 95°F with the high end being around 85°F most of the time. These animals are extremely antisocial around other chameleons and each other and should be kept singly in their own environment. They grow from 7–9 inches in length. The female lays 8–20 eggs per clutch, and will usually lay 2 clutches per year. Incubate the eggs at about 68–74°F for 7–12 months. Success has been achieved by some breeders using alternation of temperatures during the incubation. If possible, simulate spring rains at 7 months. *C. antimena* has proven to be delicate in the hands of many experienced keepers and is not recommended for the inexperienced.

Chamaeleo labordi

C. labordi is found in the southwest Madagascar forest of Kirindy and also in the western coastal region.

The habitat of this species is very similar to the above species and captive care should be the same. The female of this species when in display or warning coloration is probably one of the top three most beautiful chameleon species in the world. Her usually drab green coloration can quickly become the most electric, glowing purples and oranges with a dark background. This change has to be seen to be believed. *C. labordi* grows from 7–10 inches. The species is highly excitable and stresses easily. We have found them to be quite delicate and certainly not for the beginner. Females lay 12–18 eggs per clutch. The eggs should be incubated from 7–9 months. Simulate spring rains at 7 months.

Carpet Chameleon, *Chamaeleo lateralis major*

This species is the most common and most numerous species of chameleon found on Madagascar. It lives in a wide array of habitats favoring humid areas in the central to southern regions of Madagascar. Carpet chameleons have adapted over the ages to mountain, desert and rain forest habitats but seem to be most numerous where there is ample humidity.

C. lateralis major (major meaning a larger subspecies) has proven to be a much hardier animal than *C. lateralis* in captivity. These animals grow from 10–14 inches in overall length. Being a hardy species, the carpet chameleon will survive easily within a wide temperature range but prefers temperatures in the midseventies. Carpet chameleons like to bask in the sun and should be given the opportunity to do so. The female deposits 15–20 eggs per clutch, which should be incubated at 68–74°F for 5–7 months. They have also been hatched after a 7–9 month

Figure 7.6: Male and female *C. lateralis major*.

Figure 7.7: *C. lateralis lateralis* male.

Figure 7.8: Female *C. l. lateralis*.

incubation. Some keepers have followed alternating incubation patterns with success. Others have had equally as good results with just the normal incubation temperatures around the midseventies Fahrenheit. Simulate spring rains at 5 months. *C. lateralis* and its subspecies *C. l. major* is a quick to mature and quick to grow old and die species, having a normal life span of only a couple of years. Because it is so prolific and will produce a couple of hundred young during its lifetime, it still is worth keeping. It is

a very nice animal with interesting habits and can be kept in a smaller environment which is important to the person desiring a chameleon species for a small home. Female carpet chameleons are even more ornate and colorful than the males and are often preferred by the pet owner for this reason. They will do very well on a simple diet of medium-sized crickets, house flies that are gutloaded and other small insects, even pill bugs.

Green-eared or Malthe Chameleon, *Chamaeleo malthe*

This species is located in the northern, eastern and central regions of Madagascar and is usually found in the primary forests. The species closely resembles *C. brevicornis* but is actually more closely related to *C. cucullatus*. This species grows to a size of 10–12 inches in length. Malthe's, or green-eared chameleons as they are commonly called, have been called the Madagascar flapneck chameleon which is a common name that should be reserved for *C. brevicornis*. These animals are quite beautiful and mild in disposition. They are not frequently available and command a high price as a result, when available. They appear to like a temperature range from 55–80°F. They definitely suffer at higher temperatures.

We have owned several Malthe's and they seem to prefer higher humidity levels and drink a lot of water when it is offered. The suggested incubation temperatures is the same as for *C. lateralis*. Not much has been recorded in the literature about this species and it will require more time and experience to work out its needs in captivity. This lizard appears to be a hardy spe-

Figure 7.9: Male and female *C. malthe*.

cies and hopefully it will become established as it is a favorite of everyone who comes across it.

Chamaeleo minor

This species is located in the southcentral plateau of Madagascar. It is quite possibly the most beautiful living chameleon species, at least this can be said of the displaying female. The female's coloration is usually quite dull except when threatening a male or another imagined enemy. In display, she flashes extraordinary, vibrant electric purple, blue, orange and scarlet coloration with a dark background. It is truly breathtaking to see one of these animals in display and in captivity one is tempted to keep one of these females riled up just to enjoy the fireworks display. This species grows to a length of 7–9 inches. The male is usually twice the size of the adult female. His coloration, even when fired up, doesn't hold a candle to the females. These chameleons are reputed to be hardy in captivity and are fairly easy to reproduce. *C. minor* absolutely hates the presence of another of its own species except when breeding and even then the truce is tenuous at best. They enjoy milder temperatures of the midseventies in the vivarium and like to stay hidden in abundant plant life. *C. minor* likes a good variety of medium-sized insects and quickly tires of a monotonous diet of only crickets and mealworms. The female will lay from 10–15 eggs per clutch 3 or 4 times a year. Incubation takes 9 months with temperatures kept around the 68–74°F level. Simulate spring rain at 7 months. *C. minor* is another short-lived highly productive species that is well worth considering for the pleasure of working with such a beautiful species that is easy to breed and rear.

Oshaughnessy's Chameleon, *Chamaeleo oshaughnessyi*

Oshaughnessy's chameleon lives in the forests of the northeastern coastal regions of Madagascar and the central southern mountains. These areas are generally damp, cool forests with heavy tree cover and undergrowth. Very little seems to be known about this chameleon in nature and there is little recorded about it in literature. The animals we have cared for were very similar to Parson's chameleons in looks and behavior except that the *oshaughnessyi* were smaller and their coloration was a beautiful mottled blue and green when resting. Our animals were all very placid and did well when treated like Parson's chameleons. Everyone who saw them were impressed with how beautiful they were. This species along with most montane species seems to relish worms and land snails (dime size or smaller) in its diet. They grow up to 14 inches in length and seem to prefer a temperature range of 55–80°F along with high humidity. Our animals seemed to enjoy an early warm up in the morning sun. We

Figure 7.11: Male *C. oshaughnessyi*.

Figure 7.10: Male and female *C. minor*. *Photo: David Adamson*

Figure 7.12: Female *C. oshaughnessyi*.

presume that the incubation of this rare animal is identical to that of Parson's chameleons since they are so similar in habits. Hopefully the few people who own these magnificent creatures will propagate them for others to enjoy because they are no longer available at this time from sources in Madagascar.

Madagascar Giant or Oustallet's Chameleon, *Chamaeleo oustaleti*

This species inhabits the desert regions of Madagascar. It inhabits very dry regions where plant growth is sparse and spiny and the only available water source for months at a time is the dew that collects on the few leaves and limbs of the shrubs and trees in the area. When we first saw this chameleon imported we were not impressed as it was not as beautiful as other species of chameleons and the few animals we saw at first seemed very unhappy. Since that first experience we have completely changed our mind about these incredible animals. We purchased a captive-bred animal as a baby and

Figure 7.15: Male *C. oustaleti* large morphs.

Figure 7.16: Male *C. oustaleti* large morphs.

Figure 7.13: Gravid female *C. oustaleti* large morph.

Figure 7.17: Male smaller morph *C. oustaleti*.

Figure 7.14: Nongravid female of the large morph *C. oustaleti* on the right.

Figure 7.18: Female smaller morph *C. oustaleti* in gravid coloration.

over the years he has become an integral part of our family. We have found these animals, once acclimated, to be gentle giants who, although they aren't real socialites, demand respect from the people who know them. They aren't brightly colored like other members of the family, however a healthy female will exhibit a beautiful red netting over her brown-toned body.

There appears to be two distinct races from Madagascar. One race which is the commonly imported type reaches adulthood at a length of 15–17 inches with a body build that could be described as chunky. The other race becomes a true giant and is extremely impressive when seen as an adult. This animal reaches 2 feet in length and has the body build of a Sherman tank. We have often purchased these larger animals because they are so impressive and have had real difficulty in keeping them alive since they are so parasitized as adults. Microfilarial worms are especially prevalent in Oustalet's chameleons and we have found that the risky but necessary Ivermectin treatment holds the only real hope of deparasitizing these animals.

If you are looking for an impressive chameleon, especially when it is fully grown, then look for a breeder of this species and buy a captive-born Oustalet's; you won't be sorry. These captive-bred animals should be parasite free and will live happily for years in an open space in your home, kept on a houseplant such as a large, hanging pothos plant. Oustalet's chameleons are oblivious to dry atmosphere and hot temperatures it seems. We have exposed ours to temperatures from 40°F up to 100°F with complete impunity. In fact our Oustalet's loves to bask in an outdoor aviary when the temperatures are unbearable to other chameleons and chameleon keepers.

Females will lay 30–40 eggs per clutch annually. Under recommendation from successful breeders I pass the following information on: the incubation temperature should be about 68–74°F for a total of 9–12 months, simulate spring rain at about 7 months.

Panther Chameleon, *Chamaeleo pardalis*

This species is among the most common found

Figure 7.19: Red *C. pardalis* head shot.

Figure 7.20: Blue *C. pardalis* head shot.

on Madagascar. It inhabits the warm and humid zones of the coastline of the island as well as some of the interior areas. Even small islands surrounding Madagascar have their own color morph populations of this animal. Panther chameleons appear to have developed color morphs according to their specific locations and there are hundreds of these color pods that can be used to distinguish the general area from where the animal comes from. Subsequently, there are

Figure 7.21: Madagascar.

Figure 7.24: *C. pardalis* male captive-bred hybrid.

differences in the colorations of individual animals from the same pod. This makes identification of locale difficult. One often sees Nosy Be blue, Maroantsetra or Diego Saurez panther chameleons offered on price lists of dealers.

Figure 7.25: Possibly Nosy Tanikely sea foam green *C. pardalis*.

Figure 7.22: Male Maroantsetra red morph *C. pardalis*.
Photo: Les Brigham

Figure 7.26: Nosy Be blue *C. pardalis* female.

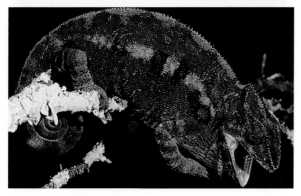

Figure 7.23: Female Maroantsetra red morph *C. pardalis*.

Figure 7.27: Male *C. pardalis* Nosy Be blue morph.
Photo: Les Brigham

Figure 7.28: Male Ambanja blue morph *C. pardalis.*

Figure 7.29: *C. pardalis* Ambanja blue morph female.
Photo: David Adamson

This generally represents the pods they are collected from. These animals are all color variations of the same species. Panther chameleons enjoy warm temperatures with a lot of humidity and are easily maintained once acclimated and deparasitized. They are aggressive and need their own living space in order to do well in captivity. We have kept several female panthers together in temporary housing without problems but I am sure they would have preferred not to be so sociable. Females can lay up to 4 clutches of eggs per year consisting of 15–35 eggs per clutch. Incubation at our farm takes 8–9 months and we keep the incubation temperature at 68–74°F during this time, simulate spring rain at 6 months. The young are easily raised together for the first 6 weeks of life when they begin fighting for territory and need to be separated.

Panther chameleons eat a wide assortment of insects and are not at all choosy about their diet. They will eat their own young or attempt to consume any other small-moving object within their area. The males are considerably larger than the females at maturity like many species

of chameleons and a full-grown male can reach 15 inches. This species is deservedly one of the most popular species as a pet and will live for many years with its owner if well cared for. The females are shorter lived then the males because they are little else then egg machines, constantly producing one clutch after another until they burn out in a couple of years. It is important to note between morphs that the females can look similar in coloration. If the reader wishes to breed panther chameleons, purchase pairs from the same locale to prevent hybridization of a color morph.

The reader can see from the photographs of the various color morphs of the panther chameleon that there are several very beautiful forms of this popular species. A little information will be of interest regarding these animals. One blue morph of *C. pardalis* is located near the east coast of Nosy Be Island a small resort island off the northern tip of Madagascar. This island is very warm year-round and has a very high level of humidity. Animals from here are somewhat different in behavior and appearance than on the mainland of Madagascar, although some animals from Ambanja are identical. We have found blue panthers to be more high strung and snappy than the other morph varieties and they do not acclimate to captivity as quickly as the others do.

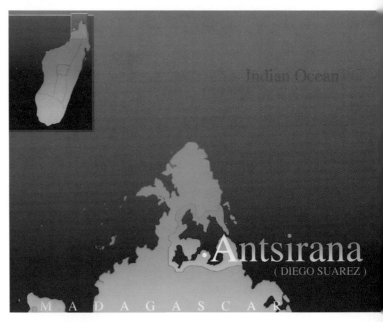

Figure 7.30: Distribution map of Diego Suarez.

Figure 7.31: Male Diego Suarez red morph *C. pardalis*.

Another color morph very similar to the Nosy Be form is the Ambanja blue panther which lives near the town of Ambanja on the island of Madagascar a short ways from Nosy Be Island.

The more often seen green morph that is commonly spotted beside the road in low-growing vegetation is located along the west coast of the island of Nosy Be and in locations on the main island of Madagascar. Its coloration is predomi-

Figure 7.32: Male green morph *C. pardalis* possibly from Nosy Be.

nantly green and white, with yellow lips on occasion. This is the morph referred to as the common panther chameleon.

There is a particularly striking red morph that comes from the east coast of Madagascar, near Maroantsetra located adjacent to the Bay of Antongila. This *C. pardalis* is usually brilliant orange-red and white during display, and a brick red or green at rest. Occasionally one of these animals will have a blue lateral stripe, and an emerald green casque, and sometimes a pure white face.

The rainbow morph (another red *C. pardalis*) hails from the northeastern region of Madagascar located near the Bay of Diego Suarez. This panther morph is green with red saddles (or vice versa), and it often displays a banana yellow underside when in full coloration. It is perhaps the most beautiful of all the morphs in my opinion and also one of the nicest in disposition.

Some breeders have bred the various morphs together and the results are often quite stunning. This practice is not true hybridization as all of the morphs are only varieties of one species and are not even subspecific, at least at this time. Recent studies indicate that the different color morphs could be different species due to variations in their genes. We would ideally like to see the morphs kept as pure as possible in captivity especially with those that are very hard to obtain. This is perhaps an impractical fantasy of ours but in the event of a natural disaster on Madagascar that could possibly wipe out a certain color morph, we would be able to reintroduce the correct and pure color morph back to this region.

Parson's Chameleon, *Chamaeleo parsonii*

Parson's chameleons live in the high cool forests of Madagascar's centraleastern mountain range and along the eastern coastal areas where there are still primary forests left. These forests are usually undisturbed regions with little logging or other manmade disasters. Parson's chameleons are shy in nature and shun areas where man has set up housekeeping. Being perhaps the most majestic chameleon of all, Parson's are in constant demand as pets and for captive-breed-

Figure 7.33: Male *C. parsonii*.

Figure 7.34: Female *C. parsonii*.

ing purposes. The adult males grow to a size of over two feet in length when mature. Some regions seem to have different races where the animals are slightly different in size, color and shape. One subspecies is called the yellow-lipped Parson's chameleon and seems to reach the greatest size within the species. Like other montane species, Parson's enjoys snails, worms, grasshoppers and will literally stand on their hind legs to reach a Madagascar giant hissing cockroach with their very long tongues. Although I have heard of captive life spans approaching twenty years I have not confirmed this. We do know that Parson's will live for many years as a well-kept pet in an air-conditioned house without benefit of direct sun rays. Our animals will flatten their bodies and tip them toward the early morning sun rays in order to get warmed up in the morning but will shun the direct warmth of the sun after this. They do not like warm sunlight after getting initially warmed up. Parson's should be kept in temperatures that fall within the range of 50–80°F and really start to suffer from the heat when the

temperatures exceed 85°F. A panting Parson's chameleon is nearing its threshold for heat tolerance and will soon suffer from a heatstroke if not cooled down. We have a friend who visited Madagascar and went to the area where Parson's chameleons live in the mountains around Perinet. He was quite surprised to find that this area often receives frosts during the wintertime and that the Parson's are unharmed by this as they go high into the trees during this time and hibernate for a couple of months each year, they are also known to dig underground at this time.

This is a species that has not been bred repeatedly and only a handful of breeders have achieved any success. It appears that the incubation time is about 15–24 months long and is probably the longest incubation period of any reptile species. The females lay one clutch of eggs per season and as a result are long lived. The normal clutch size is from 20–60 eggs with clutches in the thirties being the norm. Older, larger females seem to produce the most eggs per clutch.

Captive, male Parson's chameleons can be stimulated into breeding after a mock battle with another male that has been placed in its area or even after mirrors have been used to stimulate a singly owned male. It is also helpful to have several females for the male to choose from, as they prefer a harem. At the present time Parson's chameleons are not being allowed export status from Madagascar. I believe that the world demand for Parson's can never be filled by captive-breeding programs because most people don't have the fortitude and patience to breed this difficult species. The eggs require a room temperature of 68–74°F to develop properly and higher temperatures will cause embryos to die or be born with defects. The eggs often will not hatch all at the same time, rather they will often hatch a week or even several months apart. A egg that is not totally collapsed and molded should never be discarded. Spring rain should be simulated at 15 months.

The adults will not tolerate a low humidity situation and really like to be kept where the humidity does not go lower than 50 percent. Animals that are kept in drier situations have a hard time shedding and are chronically underweight because they absorb a lot of water from breathing in moisture through their noses. An animal kept in a drier location requires daily watering for sometimes periods of an hour. These animals will not do well when only provided with a drip system for drinking. They are not very willing to seek out a water source and because they depend on high humidity and rain falling on them in nature they must have these same conditions in captivity to thrive. A few blasts from a water atomizer will not do the trick either as these lizards will slowly dehydrate as a result of using one of these pumps. We place our animals in the bathroom shower and run the water at barely tepid temperatures for an hour at a time on low volume. This hydration method has worked well for us, as has keeping a humidifier pointed at the chameleon's tree year-round. Parson's chameleons are shy, gentle creatures and should always be handled with slow, deliberate movements, as most chameleons should be. We have been successful in keeping a group of several females together with one male for an extended period of time without much problems of stress. A large part of our success with this experiment is a result of our being able to keep our animals loose in our home with large *Ficus* trees being the center of their individual territories and vines and other limbs making aerial pathways from one region of our house to another. The animals are totally at ease with our children and dogs and the other helter-skelter of our daily lives. We hand feed them individually and have enjoyed their company very much. Parson's seem to have an intelligence above and beyond the other species of chameleons we have kept. They cannot be recommended highly enough to the person willing to give them what it takes to make them happy. At the time of publication, we have hatched 98 of these animals and have more eggs in incubation.

Madagascar Giant Spiny Chameleon, *Chamaeleo verrucosus*

Another large species that lives in the southern and southwestern region of Madagascar's famous spiny desert. The common name spiny chameleon does not come as a result of the habitat's popular name, but refers to the charac-

Figure 7.35: Male *C. verrucosus*

Figure 7.36: Female *C. verrucosus*.

teristic fringe of elongated spinelike scales that runs down the back of this chameleon.

This animal is also considered to be one of Madagascar's giant chameleons. The spiny chameleon is adapted perfectly to living in a desert that has very little rainfall throughout much of the year and where the plant life does not grow leaves during the dry periods. Evolution has provided this species with a body type that best fits this life zone, by using its slender body form more than coloration for disguise and for closely hugging the shady side of trunks of trees and shrubs during the heat of the day. Male spiny chameleons are attractively adorned in shades of pastel green edged with darker browns and tans. Often the face is sky blue and the front legs a rich orange. They are a shy species that do well in captivity but do not like to be handled very much. They have been known to grow to over 2 feet in length.

C. verrucosus prefers a temperature range of 50–100°F with the daytime temperatures at the high end and the nighttime at the lower end of the scale. Their habitat should be kept quite dry but the animals do require hydration which should be every few days.

The females of this species lay large clutches of 30–50 eggs at a time, once or rarely twice a year. Incubation is at 68–74°F for 9 months. Water should be added to the egg medium at 7 months to trigger hatching.

South African Species

Africa is the second-largest continent in the world, and divided equally from the north to south by the equator. Due to this separation, the climate of Africa is tropical both to the north and to the south. Most of the continent temperatures are warm to hot year-round except at the higher elevations. South Africa is an exception when it comes to being hot all the time. It is a country with several climatic zones and these areas vary considerably. There are basically two seasons with the winters being cool to cold and dry and the summers hot and rainy or with high humidity. There are several locations where it freezes during the wintertime and where chameleons live.

Most of the time the South African weather pattern is generally dry, where 20 percent of the country receives 8 inches or less of annual rainfall. Another 47 percent may receive 40 inches

annually, including the Natal Coast. The coast near Alexander Bay (bordering Namibia) usually receives less than 2 inches annually.

The world's most respected national parks and reserves are found in the southern and eastern nations of Africa. These include the countries of Tanzania, Zambia, Kenya, Uganda and South Africa.

Natal Midlands Dwarf Chameleon, *Bradypodion themnobates*

This dwarf species is found in the South African province of Natal. It is considered large for a dwarf species often growing to 7 inches in total length as an adult. It is also considered by many to be one of the very most attractive species. Its body shape and coloration are very beautiful and these animals deserve all of the compliments laid upon them.

This species is not normally exported from South Africa except for very stringent scientific reasons. A few years ago Bert Langerwerf the famous lizard breeder, obtained a permit and

Figure 7.38: Female *B. thamnobates*

Figure 7.37: Distribution map of South Africa.

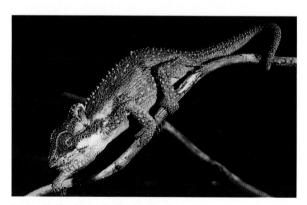

Figure 7.39: Male *B. thamnobates*.

imported some specimens from South Africa. With Bert's expertise and patience, he was soon able to breed these animals and has been very generous in supplying others with the resultant offspring.

The species is hardy in captivity and is able to endure quite a range of temperatures. Bert Langerwerf has kept them outside on a year-round basis in Alabama where the temperatures are very hot and humid during the summer and very cold with annual snow levels of over 2 feet covering the chameleons' enclosures during the winter. It is important to note that Bert has specially built his outdoor enclosures so that they are below the ground surface and are south facing. In addition, Bert covers the cages with old carpet strips during inclement weather. In nature these animals inhabit an area that is also very variable in climate.

This species is live bearing, with a gestation period of 7–9 months. They usually produce 6–20 living young per litter.

There are several other desirable species of chameleons that if available from South Africa would prove hardy in captivity. Hopefully someday these will be available also as captive-bred species.

Cameroon Species

Cameroon is located on the west coast of Africa, just north of the equator. It is bordered by Nigeria, Chad, Central African Republic, the Congo and Gabon.

Mount Cameroon which is the home area to many species of Cameroon chameleons imported into the United States is 14 miles off the coast of the Gulf of Guinea, with a height of 13,435 feet making it the highest mountain of central Africa. The city of Buea, which is one of the main collecting centers for chameleons in Cameroon, is located on the southeastern side of Mount Cameroon. This area receives about 100 inches of rainfall annually. On the mountain's west slope, rainfall can be as much as 400 inches per year, making this place one of the wettest places on earth. This mountainous region is cool (approximately 55–70°F) in the upper zones and becomes warmer as one descends

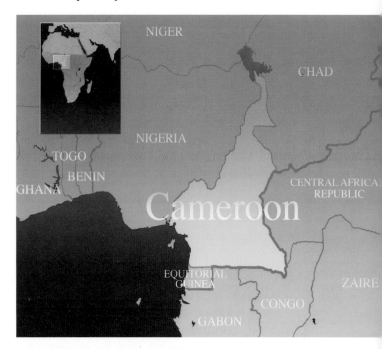

Figure 7.40: Distribution map of Cameroon.

toward the lowlands. The tropical lowland climate of Cameroon is hot and humid, with an average temperature of 70–82°F throughout the year. When one first thinks about the above climate it seems on the outside that the temperatures are quite mild and certainly not very warm by Northern Hemisphere standards. It is amazing how fast this perception changes when one first experiences travel in the Cameroon's. The heat along with the high degree of humidity quickly takes its toll on the newcomer to this region.

With 4 geographic zones, most of Cameroon is densely forested along the coast, swamp lands, volcanic peaks to the north, and isolated slopes on the border of Chad.

Two-horned Mountain Chameleon, *Chamaeleo montium*

Several mountain species of chameleons from mainland Africa exhibit a high dorsal crest or sail fin along the ridge of their backs. *C. montium* is one of these beautiful animals. The males are especially ornate with a high, thin wavy crest and two forward-pointing horns on their foreheads. This species is restricted to cooler mountain regions and is common within its habitat. It is usually collected on Mount Cameroon and even in Buea itself. The species

Figure 7.41: Male *C. montium*.

Figure 7.42: Female *C. quadricornis*.

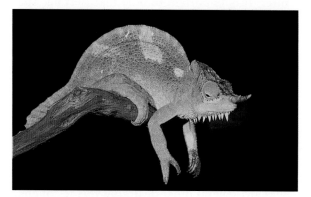

Figure 7.43: Male *C. quadricornis*.

grows to an adult size of 8–10 inches in length.

The two-horned mountain chameleon should be kept in the vivarium within a temperature range that approximates its natural environment which is between 60–75°F with winter lows to 30–40°F. Humidity should be very high approaching 100 percent but fresh air movement is also important to avoid respiratory illnesses.

The female *C. montium* usually lays 6–15 eggs per clutch 2 or 3 times per year. The eggs should be incubated at a cooler temperature of 68–74°F in a rather moist medium for a period of 4 months. Incubation temperatures can fluctuate a couple of degrees either way without affecting the embryos.

Cameroon Bearded Chameleon or Four-horned Chameleon, *Chamaeleo quadricornis*

This is another sail-finned montane species living on the Cameroon mountain ranges of Mount Manenguba and Mount Lefo. Four-horned chameleons grow to an adult length of 10–14 inches.

This cool-loving species comes from the upper regions of the rain forests covering the steep mountain slopes. It should never be exposed to temperatures exceeding 80°F for any length of time as it will quickly overheat. *C. quadricornis* loves temperatures as low as 55°F dipping to 30°F in the winter but with a high humidity. If constant humidity cannot be provided, this species will dehydrate and will eventually die from kidney failure or upper-respiratory problems. It is a species that has very exacting requirements and, when these are met, is hardy in captivity. If the chameleon keeper cannot provide for this

species' needs, then another species should be kept instead. These are among our most favorite species of chameleon and are very ornate and beautiful. They are colored in shades of forest green to dark green with lighter variations. They have a beard of elongated scales that gives them a mossy look. Although called the four-horned chameleon they sometimes can have more than 4 horns and we have seen some examples with 6 or more horns.

This species is particularly sensitive to intrusion of its environments by another chameleon even of the same species. I often hear from people who say that they can keep their *C. quadricornis* together in pairs, but sooner or later they call back with the sad news that usually the female has died or is sick and refuses to feed. This species will live quite well in captivity as long as it gets proper environmental considerations and is housed separately from all other chameleons and other reptiles and only allowed to come in contact with its own species for breeding purposes. The female will lay 10–13 eggs per clutch, 2 or 3 times per year. The eggs should be incubated for 5 months at 68–70°F in extra-moist vermiculite.

Tanzania Species

Tanzania is located on the east coast of Africa, just south of the equator. Bordered by 8 other countries, Tanzania historically boasts a fairly low human population, which in the past has allowed for the vast array of wildlife within its borders. The country envelopes many life zones and has more national parks than any other country in the world. The famous Mount Kilimanjaro is Tanzania's proudest possession.

The temperature zones vary, temperatures of the lower elevations are annually consistent, with a fluctuation only 9°F below 8000 feet. The coastal and immediate inland areas experience very high humidity year-round with an average temperature of 80°F. Rainfall averages between 30–60 inches a year.

About half the country is forested in dry acacia areas interspersed with grass plains. The remainder of the country consists of rain forests covering small mountain ranges and areas surrounding huge lakes where the landscape is primarily covered with reed and grass swamps. The central area is usually hotter and drier, with an average rainfall of 20–30 inches a year falling during the two rainy periods. Most of the species of chameleons are located in the mountain regions where it is cooler and greener. A few species do live in the lowlands and are frequently seen around villages. An example is the flap-necked chameleon, *C. dilepis*.

Fischer's Chameleon, *Chamaeleo fischeri multituberculatus*

This animal is found on the western slope of Tanzania's Usambara Mountains. It is a very hardy species both in nature and captivity and is adapted to a wide range of temperatures from 50–85°F. Fischer's chameleons live in areas where the humidity is high and in captive conditions should also be provided with this condition in mind. Animals that are not kept hydrated through high humidity or daily watering will dehydrate very quickly and are hard to bring back from death's door. These chameleons are usually heavily parasitized with a host of different species of worms and protozoans when first imported. It is very important to only purchase animals that have been treated for these prior to their sale. Usually there are losses associated with deparasitization of this species and it should be left up to the experts to purge these animals before selling them.

Females lay 15–20 eggs per clutch 2 or 3 times per year. Incubation normally takes 5–6 months at 68–74°F, add water to vermiculite at 4 months to simulate spring.

There are several subspecies of Fischer's chameleons often available and the larger montane forms seem to be particularly beautiful and hardy once acclimated.

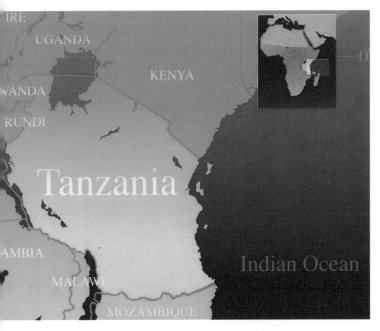

Figure 7.44: Distribution map of Tanzania.

Figure 7.45: Male and female *C. fischeri multituberculatus*.

Dwarf Mountain Three-horned Chameleon, *Chamaeleo fuelleborni*

This species is found within a very limited range located on the side of a huge volcano in Tanzania. Recent years have seen it shipped in fairly large numbers. Considering its restricted range, it's a wonder that this is still being allowed.

The species is considered small, and resembles a miniature version of Jackson's chameleon. The males sport 3 horns; both sexes are very warty and stocky in build. Fully grown a male will measure 8 inches head to tail. A very large specimen will reach 10 inches in overall length.

The Poroto Mountain Range, where this species comes from, is enshrouded in cool mists in its high altitudes and this lizard requires this cool humidity in order to survive. It is not a hardy species when compared to Jackson's chameleon which has more tolerance for drier conditions. A temperature of 50–75°F best suits this species with a humidity of around 100 percent being to its liking. If given these conditions, there is no reason this species cannot become established

in captivity. It is a desirable species to work with. When given enough room it seems to be less territorial than many other species.

These lizards are ovoviviparous (bear live young) after a gestation period of 7–9 months. They usually produce 8–15 babies per brood.

Meru Dwarf Jackson's Chameleon or Yellow-headed Jackson's Chameleon, *Chamaeleo jacksonii merumontana*

This wonderful species is located on Mount Meru the ancient sister volcano to Mount Kilimanjaro. This huge mountain is the home to several life zones with different climate areas. The rare dwarf subspecies of Jackson's chameleon is found in areas where there is cool, humid thick growth quite high up on the side of Mount Meru. The area receives torrential rain at times and cool fog throughout most of the year. The going is very rough for a hiker to reach the area where this species can be found. One collector told me that it is one of the most difficult chameleons to collect and is not worth the effort one has to expend to reach its home area. This must be one of the reasons that this species is so seldom seen in captivity along with its high price when offered from Tanzania.

This species has the same green coloration of the larger *jacksonii*, except the males bear a bright yellow head and have horns that are proportionally much longer than its giant relatives. These horns are easily broken and care should

Figure 7.46: *C. fuelleborni* female.

Figure 7.47: *C. fuelleborni* male.   Photo: David Adamson

Figure 7.48: Male and female *C. jacksonii merumontana*.

be taken not to house this species in a cage where the holes in the wire are too small, as the males will entangle their horns in it and snap them off. The females of this subspecies often display a single horn on their nose when full grown. This species will average 7 inches in overall length. The females bear living young usually with small litters but occasionally up to 20 young at a time. The females carry their young for a period of 9 months to a year depending on temperature conditions.

The vivarium for this species should be kept cool and humid with temperatures hovering around 75°F during the day and dropping at night to as low as 50°F without harm. Higher temperatures are tolerated only for short periods and these precious animals should not be allowed to endure temperatures not to their liking. Gravid females will need a place to bask in order to have their offspring develop properly inside of their bodies. Dwarf Jackson's chameleons are quite rare and very desirable to collectors and need a concentrated effort to establish them in captivity. Their present numbers in captivity are quite low and the prospect of receiving more for breeding purposes is remote.

Jackson's Chameleon, *Chamaeleo jacksonii xantholophus*

This species ranges into Tanzania in only a very few locales and is more commonly found in Kenya where it is strictly protected from collection for the trade. Several years ago this species was introduced to Hawaii when there was legal trade with Kenya in this species and the population there has expanded to several islands where it has adapted to warmer humid conditions and is thriving. Jackson's chameleons, for many years after importation was stopped, were practically impossible for a collector to obtain. But in recent years this once very rare and desirable species has been entering the trade from the Hawaiian populations and is now among the commonest species traded.

Very large male Jackson's will attain a length of 14 inches. The females are smaller and rarely bear horns except when very small, at this age they can have 3 small projections on their heads and are often mistaken for young males.

Figure 7.49: *C. jacksonii xantholophus* female.

Figure 7. 50: *C. jacksonii xantholophus* male.

Jackson's chameleons are tolerant of wide temperature swings and even tolerate temperatures exceeding 100°F for short periods of time. They are most comfortable though within the range of 55–85°F. Humidity plays a major role in the overall health of these lizards and they require a humidity range of 75–100 percent to really be happy. If the collector cannot control the higher end of the temperature range for his animals and the temperature goes above 90°F, then it is absolutely imperative to provide a humidity level of 100 percent which will enable these lizards to survive this stress more easily. We know of collectors living in the hot Arizona climate that keep Jackson's chameleons under extremely hot conditions during the summer. The trick to their success has been a constant sprinkler or misting system showering cooler water over the animals during the hottest temperatures of the day. This provides cooling as well as humidity.

These lizards are live bearing, with 20–30 babies born per brood. The gestation period is 7–9 months. Females require a basking place preferably in direct sunlight during pregnancy or the chances of stillbirth and deformed young will be quite high. The young should be removed as soon as is possible after birth because the females will eat them on occasion.

This species is one of the most desirable species of chameleons for captivity. Despite its recent ubiquity in the marketplace they are still beautiful and rewarding to keep and are a great beginner species. It should be noted here that there are several sources in Hawaii selling these animals to unsuspecting customers with the worst advice for keeping this species that we have ever heard. People are often told that these animals do not require anything special and are naturally parasite free. Often this is true, however, a fecal check is a wise idea. The reader should follow the advice given in this book for keeping their Jackson's chameleon and the animal should thrive.

Meller's Giant Chameleon, *Chamaeleo melleri*

Growing to a length of over 2 feet, this species is Africa's largest species of chameleon. It is ranked along with the Parson's and Oustalet's chameleons of Madagascar as the real giants of the chameleon world. This species is monomorphic (sexes appear the same) and very difficult to determine accurately. One breeder tells us that they can be probed to determine the sex but we have not had the opportunity to try this method yet.

This species is a tree canopy species inhabiting the cooler humid mountain regions of East Africa. It rarely descends to the ground, living its life in the trees and is rarely observed. Meller's chameleons are not for the beginner and are among the most difficult species to maintain in captivity. Most individuals perish within days to weeks after being imported and only a few specimens persist for any time at all under captive conditions. This was the story of most chameleon species only a few years ago and yet today most species are being kept with ease after they are deparasitized and kept within the parameters of their natural environments. I feel that Meller's can become established in captivity if the following factors are observed by the exporters and importers. First of all, only young and juvenile specimens should be shipped. The

Figure 7.51: *C. melleri.*

adults should be left to reproduce. These larger specimens seem to stress and collapse very quickly in captivity. The younger specimens adjust more readily to captive conditions when they are shipped fully hydrated and packed individually during shipment. Meller's chameleons are not at all sociable and show immediate stress when housed together. Certainly one of the major factors leading to their delicacy are parasites, especially blood born and protozoans. These should be attended to as soon after arrival as is possible. The newfound use of the drug Ivermectin in chameleons shows great promise when used in time to treat the parasites found in these animals. One Tanzanian shipper who understands chameleons very well ships these animals with the most success and sells only smaller, less-parasitized specimens. It is from him that most of the existing animals in captivity have come.

Meller's chameleons are delightful and deserve to be established but I fear this will have to be left up to a few dedicated individuals who have the time and expertise to perform this task. Perhaps someday captive-bred specimens will be available. It is doubtful that there is enough time to firmly establish this species before the forest home it lives in is totally gone. Meller's chameleons live in areas where deforestation is rampant. However, in many cases, Meller's have adjusted to living in the mango plantations and are actually thriving in these manmade forests.

Anyone who keeps this species should make every effort to keep it within the narrow confines of its preferred habitat requirements. Meller's chameleons require absolutely clean and fresh humid air and plenty of it. They develop upper-respiratory infections when kept differently. They like temperatures that do not exceed 90°F and can go to a lower temperature reading of 50°F at nighttime without harm.

Females lay huge clutches consisting of 30–40 eggs per clutch once a year. Incubation should be maintained at 68–74°F for a period of 4–5 months. Babies are born very large, up to 4 inches in length.

Mountain Dwarf Chameleon, *Chamaeleo rudis*

This is a species that is located in several East African countries other than Tanzania, it also can be found in Rwanda, Uganda and Zaire. It is a monomorphic species (sexes appear alike) and is difficult to determine males from females although when fully grown the males are larger than the females. *C. rudis* grows only to a length of about 6 inches and is a perfect candidate for the smaller vivarium that some collectors only have space for. This species is identical in its needs to Jackson's chameleons and can be treated the same.

This species is found in cool, moist, mountainous regions and likes a temperature range between 65–80°F. It can safely tolerate short periods of higher temperatures only when kept at a humidity level approaching 100 percent.

Being a live-bearing species like most mountainous species it can give birth to 6–12 young

Figure 7.52: *C. rudis.*

at a time once a year. The gestation period is 7–9 months.

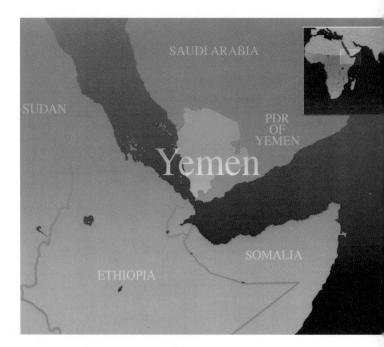

Figure 7.53: Distribution map of Yemen.

Yemen Species

Yemen is located on the southernmost tip of the Arabian Peninsula where the Red Sea and the Gulf of Aden converge. Along its coast the temperatures are more moderate with no freezing. The humidity can be high at times during the summer and the area is considered as dry, savannah land. Inland, the terrain becomes hot with low humidity and is typical Arabian desert with sparse plant life. The temperatures in this area are also typical of most deserts going from very hot during the day to cool, or downright cold, night temperatures depending on the season. In the mountains, the landscape again changes to rugged rocky escarpments hundreds of feet high, covered with desert plant life and exposed to fog conditions that water the area and make it more verdant. It is in these areas that the following species is easily located.

Veiled Chameleon, *Chamaeleo calyptratus*

C. calyptratus can be found in and around the coastal cities of Taizz and Adan as well as in the desert locations that will support it and into the

Figure 7.54: Male *C. calyptratus.*

Figure 7.55: Female *C. calyptratus.*

more moderate mountainous regions which are its true stronghold. These regions have no measurable rainfall, however the dew from the coastal humidity offers the chameleons daily water to lick from the leaves of trees and bushes. With temperatures often going above 100°F and with high humidity, these regions can be stifling.

Due to the rigors of living in this desert habitat these lizards have adapted to not only these extremes but also to the scarcity of edible insects. Apparently there are sufficient small insects for the young to grow slowly on, but once this species reaches adulthood it develops the strange and unchameleonlike habit of eating plant leaves in addition to also eating insects. Some specimens in captivity will consume up to 60 percent of their diet in vegetable matter and probably should be offered this on a regular basis. Plants that we know this species relishes are *Ficus benjamina*, broccoli, bib lettuce, romaine, dandelion and other edible weeds and occasionally some fruit. Insects will round out their diet and the adults don't seem to need many of these if given vegetable matter as a regular addition to the diet.

Young *C. calyptratus* grow extremely fast in captivity probably due to a greater abundance of food items available than what they would find in nature. This rapid and unnatural growth has cost the lives of many thousands of these captive animals because they are not supplemented with enough balanced minerals to keep their bones growing at the same rate as the rest of their bodies. We often get frantic calls concerning this condition in this species. Usually these animals have been lacking minerals far too long by the time we are contacted and are pitiful little wrecks. Metabolic bone disease is the most commonly seen anomaly in this species and could be easily avoided with proper supplementation.

Inbreeding, breeding at too young an age and improper diet is taking its toll on this species in captivity. Because veiled chameleons are so popular, many people have bought these animals with very little knowledge coming from the sellers of these animals. In fact many of the people selling their animal's offspring to others who know very little about what they are selling and often give misleading information to the new buyers. We often see and hear of females being bred at far too young an age (6 months is too young). These animals suffer tremendously from metabolic bone disease as a result of the developing eggs robbing the female's body of calcium from her bones.

This is probably the most hardy and tolerant chameleon species known. Even when a female is so weak from lack of bone mass and from being overfed and grown too fast she will still survive, even if unable to walk or stay on a branch she will persist.

Veiled chameleons for all of their popularity are certainly one of the most unpleasant animals to own. Occasionally a specimen can be found that at least does not try to bite when picked up. These more tractable animals are usually raised singularly from birth and have had constant attention and handling from their owners. If this is something the reader can dedicate himself to then he will find this species still standoffish but very interesting just the same.

Males of this species grow to 18–24 inches in length. They can be kept in temperatures that range from 45–100°F but should be kept at lower temperature ranges around 85°F. Humidity is much appreciated and watering by sprinkling or heavily misting is necessary.

C. calyptratus will lay several large clutches of eggs per year. Usually clutches consist of 25–30 eggs and overfed females will produce even larger clutches that endanger their lives and certainly shorten them. Incubate the eggs for 7–9 months at 68–74°F. If a female is allowed to produce a couple of clutches per year then given a rest period, she will live longer and produce eggs over a greater amount of time. This rest can be induced by lowering the ambient temperature during our wintertime so that the female is not kept at constantly warmer temperatures. I recommend that the female, and for that matter the male, also be cooled down to temperatures in the low sixties at night with the temperature raised up to the midseventies during the daytime. A basking area for warming their bodies during the daytime is beneficial. Any animals that have a health condition such as upper-respiratory infection should not be cooled. Animals should be gradually exposed to this regimen over a couple of weeks or a month. The temperatures should not be lowered over a short period of time like a day or two, as this might result in inducing an upper-respiratory infection. The animals should be kept in this cooling period for a period of 2–3 months during which time they will slow down on their needs for food and will become a lot less active. When the time for warming comes it should be done as gradually as the cooling period was.

Glossary

APPENDAGE: an extension of the body diverging from the axial trunk such as the legs or nose.

ASPIRATE: to fill the lungs with fluid, possibly causing death.

BULBOUS: round or bulb-shaped.

DEPOSITORY: a place to deliver or leave eggs (in captivity a depository could be a soil floor for digging, a potted plant or a soiled-filled trash can).

DIAPAUSAL PHASE: a period of growth cessation due to a cooling of temperatures.

FECAL: pertaining to or being feces.

FECES: waste matter discarded from the intestines through the anus.

GAPE: to open its mouth.

GRAVID: pregnant.

GULAR: the upper part of the throat.

HEMIPENIS: a two-sided penis where the sperm travels on the exterior surface into the vent of the female.

MONTANE: pertaining to mountain regions.

ROSTRAL PROCESS: pertaining to the protuberances on the end of the nose (paddle or hornlike appendage).

PERLITE: a volcanic glass, usually appearing as a mass of enamel-like balls.

PHOSPHOROUS: containing trivalent phosphorous or phosphor.

PREHENSILE TAIL: a tail adapted for seizing or grasping.

PURGE: to rid of whatever is impure or undesirable.

SHED: to cast off or let fall by a natural process, usually pertaining to the skin in chameleons.

THERMAL REGULATE: the ability to regulate one's own temperature.

TOURNIQUET: a band that restricts blood flow to a specific body part.

VENT: the anal or excretory opening of animals such as birds or reptiles, also the sexual opening.

VERMICULITE: any group of platy minerals, hydrous silicates of aluminum, magnesium and iron that expand upon being heated.

Bibliography

Branch, Bill. *Field Guide to the Snakes and Other Reptiles of Southern Africa*. Ralph Curtis Books, 1988.

The British Herpetological Society Bulletin. # 27. 1989.

————. #45. 1993.

Encyclopaedia Britannica, vols. 3, 14, 26, 27.

Frye, Frederic L., D.V.M. *Reptile Care an Atlas of Diseases and Treatments*, vols. 1 and 2. T.F.H. Publications Inc., 1991.

Klingenberg, Roger, D.V.M. *Understanding Reptile Parasites*. Advanced Vivarium Systems, 1993.

Martin, James. *Masters of Disguise*. Facts on File.

Preston-Mafham, Ken. *Madagascar, A Natural History*. Facts on File, 1991.

Roberts, Martin F. *All about Chameleons and Anoles*. T.F.H Publications, Inc. Ltd., 1981.

Schnieper, Claudia. *Chameleons*.

Stahl, Scott J., D.V.M. *Veterinary Management of Indoor Collections of Chameleons*. 18th International Herpetological Symposium, Program and Abstracts, 1994.

Appendix

Temperature

Celsius = Fahrenheit
8 = 46.40
9 = 48.20
10 = 50.00
11 = 51.80
12 = 53.60
13 = 55.40
14 = 57.20
15 = 59.00
16 = 60.80
17 = 62.60
18 = 64.40
19 = 66.20
20 = 68.00
21 = 69.80
22 = 71.60
23 = 73.40
24 = 75.20
25 = 77.00
26 = 78.80
27 = 80.60
28 = 82.40
29 = 84.20
30 = 86.00
31 = 87.80
32 = 89.60
33 = 91.40
34 = 93.20
35 = 95.00
36 = 96.80
37 = 98.60
38 = 100.40
39 = 102.20

Weights and Measurements

Millimeters		Centimeters		Inches
76.20	=	7.62	=	3.00
88.90	=	8.89	=	3.50
101.60	=	10.16	=	4.00
114.30	=	11.43	=	4.50
127.00	=	12.70	=	5.00
139.70	=	13.97	=	5.50
152.40	=	15.24	=	6.00
165.10	=	16.51	=	6.50
177.80	=	17.78	=	7.00
190.50	=	19.05	=	7.50
203.20	=	20.32	=	8.00
215.90	=	21.59	=	8.50
228.60	=	22.86	=	9.00
241.30	=	24.13	=	9.50
254.00	=	25.40	=	10.00

Key

kg = kilogram = 1000 grams = 2.2 lbs
mg = milligram = .001 grams
ml = milliliter = .001 liters
SQ = subcutaneous (under the skin)
IM = intramuscular
PO = per os (by mouth)

Insect Suppliers

These listings of food insect suppliers and biological supply houses are provided for your convenience, as most new chameleon owners do not have access to this information.

BASSET'S CRICKETS
 Crickets
  (800) 634-2445
  535 N. Lovers Lane
  Visalia, CA 93291

THE BIOLOGY STORE
 Fruit flies
  (619) 745-1445
  P.O. Box 2691
  Escondido, CA 92033

GHANN'S CRICKET FARM, INC.
 Crickets
 Mealworms
  (800) 476-BAIT
  Box 211840
  Augusta, GA 30917-184

GRUBCO INC.
 Waxworms
 Mealworms
 Giant mealworms
 Fly larvae
  (800)222-3563
  Box 15001–0001
  Hamilton, OH 45015

JA-DA BAIT
 Waxworms
 Fly larvae
 (This is the only source of the large timber Antigo fly larvae we have found.)
  (715) 627-4648
  P.O. Box 217
  Antigo, WI 54409-0217

RAINBOW MEALWORMS
 Crickets
 Mealworms
 Giant mealworms
 Fly larvae
 Waxworms
  (800) 777-9676
  126 Spruce St.
  P.O. Box 4907
  Compton, CA 90220
  213-227-6566

TRIPLE-R-CRICKET RANCHES
 Crickets
 Giant mealworms
  (209) 651-2400
  P.O. Box 935
  Visalia, CA 93279

Biological Supply Houses

CAROLINA BIOLOGICAL SUPPLY
  (800) 334-5551
  2700 York Rd.
  Burlington, NC 27215

INSECT LORE PRODUCTS
 Praying mantis
 Silkworms
  (800) LIVE-BUG
  P.O. Box 1535
  Shafter, CA 93263

SPECIAL CARE PET CENTER
 Madagascar hissing cockroaches
 Praying mantis
  (412) 928-9433
  5 West Prospect Avenue
  Pittsburgh, PA 15205

Index